A Southern Story

A Southern Story

Family and Race, ca. 1650–2021

Sterling Vinson

RESOURCE *Publications* · Eugene, Oregon

A SOUTHERN STORY
Family and Race, ca. 1650–2021

Resource Publications
An Imprint of Wipf and Stock Publishers
199 W. 8th Ave., Suite 3
Eugene, OR 97401

www.wipfandstock.com

PAPERBACK ISBN: 978-1-6667-3666-3
HARDCOVER ISBN: 978-1-6667-9536-3
EBOOK ISBN: 978-1-6667-9537-0

APRIL 20, 2022 2:27 PM

Material from *The Embattled Ladies of Little Rock* by Vivon Lenon Brewer (copyright 1999 by Patricia Murphey Rostker) is reproduced by permission of Lost Coast Press, www.cypresshouse.com.

Scripture quotations from The Authorized (King James) Version. Rights in the Authorized Version in the United Kingdom are vested in the Crown. Reproduced by permission of the Crown's patentee, Cambridge University Press

Dedicated to my parents,
Louise Estelle Scott and James Russell Vinson,
and to
Mr. Julius Cherry, teacher and mentor

Contents

List of Illustrations

As I was preparing the manuscript for publication, it hit me forcibly that one result of my family's racism is that I have no photographs of any of the people of color who worked so hard for us and shared our lives for so long. Bessie, Julius, and the Tanabes have vanished from our records without a trace. Fortunately, Mae Tanabe's daughter, Lynn, has photographs of her parents taken about that time. I dimly remember as a child taking a stiffly posed photograph of Julius, but it is long gone, and as fond as I was of Bessie, I never took a picture of her. I am saddened, and I apologize.

Acknowledgements

I FIRST want to thank John Fife, former pastor, and the congregation of Southside Presbyterian Church in Tucson, who gave me a sense of calling at a time when I needed it. So did Jim and Pat Corbett of Pima Friends Meeting. Pastor Alison Harrington of Southside continues the call. Rev. Robin Hoover, sometime pastor of First Christian Church, founded Humane Borders and continues to fight for justice on the border. Frank Flasch, Leslie "Buzz" Davis, and Gregory McNamee—former student, writer, translator, and editor—encouraged me to form a blog into a book. Rev. John Ross of Southside pointed me to just the right publisher, thus saving me months of frustrating searching. Pima Community College hired me for many years to continue my education by teaching.

My wife, Mary Kierzek, teacher, painter, and musician, keeps alive the memory of the forgotten in their portraits and in their songs. I owe her more than I can express.

My daughters traveled through the South with me. Aylwyn spent dozens of hours digitizing the large family photo archive and constructing a genealogy; Vivion and my son-in-law Dr. Babak Ashrafi dealt with my endless questions about technology and recalibrated the photographs to meet the publisher's standard.

Lynn Tanabe Grannan graciously allowed me to use photographs of her parents.

Introduction

IT is August 22, 2020, and from my home in Tucson, Arizona, I am watching my country disintegrate. First, we have the appallingly racist and almost certainly illegal treatment of immigrants and refugees, chiefly from Latin America and Haiti, but not a few from Africa. This includes the separation of parents from children, the imprisonment of all in inhumane conditions, and the deportation of thousands without an adequate hearing. All of this is very similar to Mussolini's treatment of Jews from 1938 on.[1]

Second, the novel COVID-19 virus has killed about 170,000 people in the past six months and shows every sign of getting worse.[2] President Trump first tried to deny that the virus would be a problem, but when it became clear that it was a terrible problem, his comments suggested that the individual states would have to deal with it as best they could.[3] States are struggling to meet the challenges of the pandemic with limited federal funding, which "has pitted some governments against one another, forcing them

1. See Zucotti, *Italians and the Holocaust*, chap. 3.

2. McGraw, "170,000 COVID Deaths." Over 700,000 as of November 1, 2021 (Bosman and Leatherby, "U.S. Coronavirus Death Toll").

3. On December 31, 2020, for example, after continually minimizing the seriousness of COVID-19, he said, "The Federal Government has distributed the vaccines to the states. Now it is up to the states to administer. Get moving!" On April 1, 2020, Trump commented the following about governors who were begging the federal government for ventilators and medical equipment to handle COVID-19 hospitalizations: "They have to treat us well, also. They can't say, 'Oh, gee, we should get this, we should get that'" (Doggett, "Trump's Coronavirus Responses").

to scrap over the fast-dwindling, limited aid."[4] There is no plan; testing is minimal and ineffective, with the result that contact tracing is almost useless; and many people (acting on the example of ignorant and cowardly government officials) refuse to wear masks or to be vaccinated.

Third, that plague arrived when we were already suffering from an epidemic of what doctors call "deaths of despair": a startling rise in alcoholism, drug addiction, obesity, and suicide.[5] Young people are told that college is necessary for the good life, but fewer and fewer people can afford it; those who can afford it graduate with huge debt. People fall prey to these diseases because of the poverty and hopelessness of their lives. They see no way out of dead-end jobs at low wages and rising prices, lack of medical care, substandard housing and schooling, and the self-blame that goes along with those problems. An article from May states that online alcohol sales have gone up by 234 percent during the pandemic.[6]

Fourth is the racial violence fostered and exemplified by the Trump administration.[7] In February, Trump dispatched armed Border Patrol Tactical Unit (BORTAC) teams to cities that had declared sanctuary—those that had ordered their local police not to cooperate with federal immigration authorities in defiance of Trump's policy.[8] Then, city police and White vigilantes around the country disgrace us all by murdering unarmed citizens of color, notably George Floyd, Breanna Taylor, and twenty-year-old Daunte Wright, to name only three of many. This is nothing new, but a rash of particularly brutal killings filmed by security cameras and private citizens has been publicized on social media, most notably the video of George Floyd's murder filmed by Darnella Frazier.[9] The consequent protests by a citizenry already inflamed

4. Romm and Werner, "Local Governments," para. 1.

5. Healy, "Suicides and Overdoses," para. 9.

6. "Rebalancing," para. 9.

7. See Cobb, "Donald Trump."

8. Pilkington, "These Are His People," para. 18. See also Cooke and Hesson, "'Sanctuary' Cities."

9. See Nevett, "George Floyd."

by the cruel treatment of immigrants have driven the executive branch of government to send unidentified armed forces dressed in camouflage (Border Patrol? military?) to Portland, Oregon, where they have arbitrarily snatched unoffending citizens off the street into unmarked cars.[10] In Washington, DC, Trump used the armed forces and police to violently break up an otherwise peaceful demonstration in Lafayette Square between St. John's Episcopal Church and the White House, thus equating Christianity with racial violence.[11]

At the time of the writing of this book, the government is sending these armed paramilitaries to Chicago and Albuquerque. These tactics are analogous to Hitler's SA and Mussolini's Blackshirts.[12] Such goon squads provoke violence—under protest from the mayors and governors—and then brutally beat, arrest, and intimidate ordinary citizens, thus subverting legitimate local civil authority.[13]

I write now on 23 September 2021, over nine months after Trump incited a mob to attack the US Capitol in order to interfere with the Electoral College. Yesterday (September 16) he indirectly incited supporters to move on the Capitol, protesting the arrests and indictments of their brethren. In the end, nothing happened. President Joe Biden is now using armed and mounted Border Patrol agents to brutalize thousands of unarmed Haitians trying to enter the United States by crossing the Rio Grande River at Del Rio, Texas.[14] His special envoy to Haiti has resigned in protest.[15]

Trump hired Louis DeJoy, a wealthy donor, as postmaster general. DeJoy has busied himself removing mailboxes and mail sorters, eliminating overtime, and issuing orders that employees should just quit at quitting time, leaving unsorted mail on the floor to be dealt with the next day. DeJoy then stated that the post office

10. Levinson et al., "Federal Officers."

11. See Gelles et al., "Police Pushed Aside Protestors."

12. See Zucotti, *Italians and the Holocaust*, chap. 3.

13. Fox, "U.S. Agents."

14. See Chappell, "Border Agents Chased Migrants."

15. Jakes and Sullivan, "Diplomat to Haiti Resigns."

will probably be unable to deliver all of the mail-in ballots on time during the November election, so that large numbers, he said, might go uncounted![16]

Furthermore, in hearings before Congress, DeJoy stated exactly the contrary—that all ballots would be delivered on time, despite his refusal to replace the mail sorters.[17] Congress so far appears to have ignored this contradiction. It is obvious that Trump wants to sabotage mail-in voting ahead of the election in November. Mail-in voting is especially important for this election, because many people are afraid to go to the polls, where they risk infection by the COVID-19.[18] Biden has inexplicably kept DeJoy in office.

The descent of the US into this kind of fascism has been a lengthy process which I have described elsewhere,[19] but Trump has speeded it up and has even hinted at the assassination of Hilary Clinton.[20]

Of these problems, racism and alcoholism resonate with me most. As a privileged (i.e., well-to-do) White male born in Arkansas long before the Civil Rights and Voting Rights Acts, I have been dealing with racism from the oppressor's side all my life, struggling to free myself. Besides, I am a recovering alcoholic, having sobered up forty-two years ago.

There has been much talk in recent years of the need to have a national conversation about race. White folk in particular are being urged to face honestly the appalling depth and extent of racism in all areas of our national life. And we are urged to get honest not just in an abstract way but to sit down with folks of different colors and to learn from them.

16. See Woodward, "Dejoy's Postal Service."

17. McCausland, "DeJoy Testifies before Congress."

18. As it happened, the presidential election of 2020 was one of the best regulated, most tightly controlled, and fairest elections in recent history, much to the disgust of the right wing of the Republican Party. The silliness of the Republican recount in Maricopa County, Arizona, has gained national attention.

19. See Vinson, "Fascism Creeps Up."

20. Smith, "Donald Trump." For a long, perceptive piece on related subjects, see Freedman, "Angry, Armed Americans."

This memoir is an attempt to do just that: to be as honest as I can with whomever might read it. But it is more than just another family history. Because it begins in the late seventeenth century and is located almost entirely in the South, it covers almost the whole history of the southern English colonies and the Southern United States over a period of almost four hundred years. I have, therefore, tried to give as much historical and social context as I can. Because it is about the South and because we today live in a critical, kaleidoscopic period of White relations with people of color, I focus on those relationships not as an apology (none can ever be adequate) but simply to say that I am aware of—I acknowledge—what my family and my country have done.

I tell two stories, really. One is the story of my childhood in Arkansas, what that society was like, and how I believe that we have changed or not changed over the last eighty-odd years. The other story, interleaved with the first, is my slow discovery of my family's and (consequently) my nation's history. I tell the second story not in chronological order but in the order of discovery, so as to provide historical and social context for my personal story. The result is sometimes messy, like the lives of the people who lived it. They were my family, so I cannot but own them, even when I wish that they, and I, had done things differently.[21]

---

21. I am deeply indebted to an old family friend, Harry Ashmore, longtime editor of the *Arkansas Gazette*, the oldest newspaper west of the Mississippi. See his *An Epitaph for Dixie* and *Arkansas*, a guide published for the bicentennial of the United States. The latter especially explores how Arkansas's failure to resolve the contradiction between justice and White supremacy has become recognized today as a national failure (see Ashmore, *Arkansas*, xix–xx).

Chapter 1

Geography and Politics

T HE state of Arkansas is divided. Its shape is almost square, with a little piece taken out of the northeast corner by Missouri, and another little piece taken out of the southwest corner by Texas. The Mississippi River long ago took a thin northeast-southwest slice off the eastern edge, and kept nibbling away at that until the Corps of Engineers built the modern levees in the late 1920s.

My home town, Little Rock, the capital, lies almost at the center of the state, precisely on a geologic divide running northeast—southwest across the city and the state, between the southern and eastern flatlands and the western and northern Ouachita and Ozark Mountains.

On the other hand, the Arkansas River (which rises in Colorado) enters the state at Fort Smith, slightly to the northwest of Little Rock, and empties into the Mississippi River near Arkansas Post, somewhat to the southeast of the capital. These two features, the mountains and the river, are like an X across the face of the state.

This division between hills and plain had a profound effect on the Whites who came to live there in the late seventeenth century and after. By the time Arkansas became a state in 1836, the settlers in the eastern plains were growing cash crops like cotton with slave labor. Those in the hills had little use for slaves, but lived on subsistence farms and hunted. When the Civil War broke out, Arkansas, like all the Confederate states except for Florida, sent substantial numbers of troops to the Union as well as to the Confederacy.[1] No wonder the latter's president, Jefferson Davis, lamented that the epitaph of the Confederacy might well be "Died of a theory."[2]

This is not to say that Arkansas's mountaineers believed in the equality of the African American—far from it. But because there were so few Blacks in that part of the state, violence against them was sporadic and disorganized compared to the large-scale, systematic oppression (by, for example, the Ku Klux Klan) in flat plantation country, where cheap African American labor was vital to the economy.

When my parents married in 1931, my maternal grandfather, Scott, gave them twelve acres of pine and oak on the slope of the first real hill that one encounters west of Memphis, 140 miles away. There, on the edge of the fault line that runs across the whole state, they built a big white house in Georgian style, complete with a front porch imitating a porte cochere and a fanlight over the door. "I love Georgian architecture," gushed one visitor. "You know, I'm from Georgia."

The Georgian Home, long after sale

1. Ashmore says it was five thousand, a good-sized brigade at the time (Ashmore, *Arkansas*, 79).

2. Rael, "Died of a Theory."

When I lived there between my birth in 1939 and going to prep school in Vermont in 1954, this geologic fault marked a class and racial boundary as hard as the underlying rock. Wealthy people like us who lived on the hills had a fantastic view of the Arkansas River, the cliffs of Big Rock on the opposite side, and the business district of the city a few miles away. At night, the glittering lights provided their own spectacle, mirroring the stars. In those days, the city was so small (eighty-nine thousand in 1940[3]) that we, several miles from downtown, could still see the Milky Way. Saint Augustine might have thought of the City of Man and the City of God in such a place.

Below our house in the floodplain was the ghetto called West Rock. There lived the African American "help": the maids and cooks, the men of all work (called "yard boys," regardless of age). These trudged up the hill along an abandoned wagon road through the oak and pine woods every day to the back doors of the White people's houses, where they cooked, cleaned, tended the White children, and manicured the gardens and lawns of the wealthy Whites. I don't know what the wages were—something in the order of a dollar a day, I think, which was too much to starve on but not enough to support a family in decency or comfort. West Rock caught the runoff of rainwater from high ridges to the south and west. It flooded with every rainstorm because it had no sewer system.

I want to dispel immediately the dishonest, romanticized picture of Black-White relations shown in movies like *The Help*.[4] Race relations were closer to those shown in *To Kill a Mockingbird*. Even there, the Black defendant charged with raping a White woman was extremely lucky to escape lynching long enough to go to trial, as demonstrated by the murder of Emmett Till and as I shall show again in the last chapter. In the South during the period I'm talking about and for decades after, a Black employee who served a dung pie to her White employer (as an African American maid does in the movie) would have been killed, her family would have been

---

3. Federal Writers' Project, *Arkansas*, 169.
4. Taylor, *Help*.

killed, their house would have been burned, and their neighborhood would have been lucky to escape a pogrom. Segregation, like slavery before it, was always based on sudden, overwhelming, state-sanctioned violence.

If you were born and lived in the South after the Civil and Voting Rights Acts of 1964 and 1965, you can have no idea of what segregation was like. I'm White, so I have only a shadowy idea of what it was like for Black people, and much of that I have learned from constant study.

There have been two civil rights eras in the United States. One was 1863–77. In 1863, the Emancipation Proclamation became effective; 1877 was the end of Reconstruction, when the last federal troops left Florida, the last former Confederate state still occupied. The US then allowed Southern Whites to snatch away all the many and substantial gains that Blacks had made in fourteen years.

In 1955, when I was a sophomore in high school, C. Vann Woodward published *The Strange Career of Jim Crow*.[5] The book was startling at the time, because it demonstrated that segregation was not an eternal verity in the US, dating perhaps from colonial times, but an invention of the late nineteenth century.

Woodward points out that before 1877, segregation by race was sporadic at most. Well-to-do White Southerners were accustomed to traveling with their Black valets, lady's maids, and nannies. When, after the Civil War, former Confederate General Hood, commander of the famous Texas Brigade, traveled with his wife, eleven children, and a couple of servants, hotel staff would cry, "Here comes Hood's Brigade!"[6] Whites expected their servants to be close at hand, so trains, for example, had to put them in the same cars as their bosses.

Of course, few Blacks could afford to pay their own train fare or stay in hotels and eat at restaurants in the 1870s and '80s, so the issue was largely moot. But in 1877, Rutherford B. Hayes won the presidency by promising to pull the last federal troops (and the Freedman's Bureau) out of the South. With the removal of Union

5. Woodward, *Strange Career*.
6. Dyer, *Gallant Hood*, 315.

coercion, Southern Whites were free to grasp at political power again, without the embarrassing violence of the Ku Klux Klan.[7] Over the next generation, they passed laws to suppress the Black vote, just as Whites all over the country are doing today. Grandfather clauses stated that one could vote if his grandfather had voted (which eliminated former slaves and descendants of slaves) and instituted poll taxes, a fee for voting. The poll tax was one dollar, which speaks volumes about the dire economic condition of Blacks then, who found it hard to scrape together and spend a whole dollar all at once, when their children were hungry.

Whites also instituted White primary elections and literacy tests, demanding that semiliterate or illiterate field hands read and explain a portion of the US Constitution.[8] Have you ever tried to explain the Electoral College to someone? These restrictions were followed by a myriad of local laws segregating everything from color-coded drinking fountains to hotels, public transit, swimming pools, and what Harry Ashmore called the "last seat" of White supremacy, public toilets.[9]

In 1896, the US Supreme Court drove the final nail into the coffin of the first civil rights era with its decision in Plessy v. Ferguson. This set forth the pernicious doctrine of "separate but equal." Of course, the decision ignored the fact that separation implies inequality. Thus, states could maintain separate schools, for example, as long as they were equal. But, of course, the schools never were equal, because White state legislatures never appropriated nearly as much money for Black children as they did for Whites. In public transportation, even in interstate commerce, passenger cars for Blacks were in poor condition compared to those for Whites, and so on. There was no federal enforcement mechanism for the "equal" part of the decision, so segregation—separate and

7. Eric Foner remarks that pro-Union Southerners evaded Confederate military service and became postwar Republican leaders of Reconstruction, but often were nevertheless White supremacists—the ancestors and nucleus of Strom Thurmond's Dixiecrats, Nixon's Southern Strategy, and (I would add), Trump's base (Foner, *Reconstruction*, 16–17). See below, pp. 9, 10.

8. Dinnerstein et al., *Natives and Strangers*, 229.

9. Ashmore, *Epitaph for Dixie*, 124.

unequal—remained the law of the land throughout the nation until the Truman and Eisenhower administrations in the late 1940s and '50s.[10]

A family story about a long-dead second cousin named Exum Vinson (the third of that name) may give a sense of the racial climate of Arkansas in the 1920s. When they were teens in Augusta, Arkansas (a village about forty miles north of Little Rock), according to Cousin Katherine, her brother Ekky (as she called him) came running into the house one day and grabbed his rifle. Of course, Katherine was alarmed and asked him what was up. He yelled that an African American (not his words) had stolen his skiff and was paddling across the White River. Katherine tackled him, but he tickled her to make her let go and ran to the riverbank to shoot the thief. An elderly man counseled, "Let him go, sonny. He's headed for the canebrake, and the cottonmouths will get him for sure." The White River is quite wide at that point, and Exum was out of breath from running, which made it difficult to aim a rifle, so he held his fire.

I like to think that no one in the story, perhaps not even Ekky, really wanted to kill the Black man. Probably, Ekky just thought that it was expected of him. While an all-White and probably all-male jury would have acquitted him, it would have been a sorry thing to have on his conscience at such a young age. But that the boy could even consider such a thing speaks volumes about Black-White relations and the violence underlying them.

10. See Zinn, *People's History*, chap. 9.

Chapter 2

History, Race, and Childhood

THE second civil rights era began in 1948, when President Truman ordered the integration of the armed forces by Executive Order 9981. That proceeded slowly and still had problems when I was on active duty in the early '60s (see below, p. 42).

Nevertheless, we had the draft, not the all-volunteer force of today, so all able-bodied adult males (women weren't drafted then) of all colors and classes had to get used to eating, training, and sleeping side by side and, two years after Truman's order, fighting and dying together in Korea.

In 1954, the Supreme Court ordered the public schools to integrate in Brown v. Board of Education of Topeka, Kansas. The next two years saw the bus boycott in Montgomery, Alabama. Finally, in 1964 and 1965, people of color were allowed full civil rights and to vote.

The second civil rights era may be said to have begun its decline after our retreat from Vietnam in 1973, when we ended ground operations. In that year, President Nixon ended the draft, because he was facing an election (not to mention the scandal of Watergate) and too many White boys from rich and middle-class families were getting killed, thus further imperiling Nixon's chances for reelection. Going from the draft to an all-volunteer force means that poor people, especially poor people of color, enlist in disproportionate numbers, while middle- and upper-class Whites dodge to college or, like Trump, cadge medical excuses.

But the bitter end of that era came in 2013, when the US Supreme Court handed down its decision to effectively nullify the Voting Rights Act in the case of Shelby County v. Holder. The Voting Rights Act had specified, among other things, that states with a history of racial discrimination in voting laws (e.g., poll taxes, literacy tests, etc.) had to allow citizens of every color to vote without those impediments, had to change or abolish their old laws, and could not make any further changes to their voting laws without approval by the US attorney general. For all practical purposes, the states in question had belonged to the Confederacy, but several other states were included as well (Arizona among them). In its decision, the Supreme Court held, without any supporting evidence and in the face of abundant evidence of voter suppression by Republicans, that the restrictions of the Voting Rights Act were no longer necessary. The result is that the states can, theoretically, impose any restrictions they like, and are now doing so with enthusiasm.

Shelby County v. Holder takes us back to a repetition of 1877, even before Plessy v. Ferguson in 1896. With the withdrawal of federal protection, in the absence of a declared federal civil rights policy, the result has been a flood of state laws restricting voting all over the country, with a tsunami of restrictive laws[1] since Trump lost to Biden in 2020. These laws are promoted by Republicans. It is difficult to conclude that the majority of the justices on the Supreme Court (three of whom were nominated by Trump) and the Republican state legislators and governors who pass these laws are anything but racist.[2]

---

1. According to the Brennan Center for Justice at New York University, 361 of these bills were introduced across the nation (Knappenberger, "Arizona Near Top," para. 7).

2. Simon and Stevenson mention that Daniel Drezner, a scholar of international relations, has likened the Republican Party to Hezbollah, "a political party that also has an armed wing to coerce other political actors through violence" (Simon and Stevenson, "How Can We Neutralize," 34).

Perhaps this is a good place to explain Dixiecrats and Nixon's Southern Strategy, which I mentioned in note 7 on page 5, above. When I was around twelve, I asked my Aunt Anne (who had married my Uncle Baldy Jr.[3]) what party she belonged to. She replied that she was a Dixiecrat. I had no idea what that meant. Indeed, I had no idea what it meant to belong to a party, but I figured that because the word had Dixie in it and we lived in Dixie, it must be a good thing. Boy, was I wrong, but of course, I was just a child.

The South of my fathers had been based on cotton (or tobacco and rice where they would grow), White supremacy, and the Democratic Party (or its equivalent) since colonial times. This was "the solid South." When Democrat President Truman (notably from the border state of Missouri) integrated the armed forces and took other actions to further civil rights in 1948, radical Democrats began looking around for a party and leadership that would protect White supremacy. They found a leader in Governor Strom Thurmond of South Carolina and so broke ranks with the mainline Democrats to form the Dixiecrats. When his term as governor expired, Thurmond won a seat in the US Senate in 1954 and kept it for the next forty-eight years!

Although Thurmond became a Republican in 1964 and the Dixiecrats ceased to exist as a political party almost as soon as it was created, the sentiments and personalities of men like Thurmond did untold damage to all peoples' civil rights for two generations.

President Richard Nixon's Southern Strategy, in brief, dates to the mid-sixties and was a Republican plan to win Democratic votes for the Republicans by appealing to White racism—i.e., by winning over people like Thurmond. Nixon did this by using "dog whistle" terms such as "law and order" at a time when African Americans were actively demonstrating and speaking out against White racism, breaking the color bar, and using crack cocaine instead of the more expensive powder favored by Whites (Nixon started the War on Drugs officially in 1971). It worked, of course, and Nixon won his second presidential election before foundering

---

3. The second of that name. It was their legal, baptismal name.

on the rocks of Watergate and corruption charges too numerous to mention.

Nevertheless, it is clear that such people are the core of Trump's base today, with, as Foner notes, a history going back to Reconstruction Southerners who favored the Union but were nevertheless White supremacists.

I fervently hope that today (now 24 April 2021) the United States is entering a third civil rights era sparked by the Black Lives Matter movement. That depends on its duration and achievements. Body-camera footage and mass, instant distribution of videos of police violence against Blacks have aroused public revulsion and a demand for legal remedies. But the nation is more deeply divided now than I ever remember, so it will be correspondingly harder to bring about lasting change. Two bills, HR 1 and S 1, designed to correct the foolish injustice of Shelby County v. Holder await action in their respective chambers of Congress, but passage of either in a Senate with a margin of one Democratic vote is very questionable. If they fail, President Biden may take executive action, but this is purely speculative.

White people born in the South before the second civil rights era suffer to a greater or lesser degree from a delusional view of people of color, especially of Black people. Foner cites a former slave owner who wrote after the war, "I believed that these people were content, happy, and attached to their masters," an attitude that slaves (and later free Blacks) worked hard to foster in order to deflect White suspicions.[4] The slave owner cited by Foner contrasts sharply with Mary Chestnut, who feared a slave revolt during the whole of the war, a telling difference of gender.[5]

Daily life under segregation meant that Blacks and Whites mingled on the most intimate terms: our Black maids, Old Pearl and New Pearl, fed me and changed my diapers, and when I was older, Julius, our yard "boy," taught me all manner of things about kindness and chores that need to be done around the house. They were, as far as I could tell, created equal, but society and the Constitution

---

4. Foner, *Reconstruction*, 10–11.

5. Woodward, *Mary Chestnut's Civil War*.

said that they weren't and made sure that all of us obeyed the lie (even if we had doubts about it), just so we could get across town on the bus.

In about 1942, when she was ten, my sister, Lynn, boarded a city bus. The rule was that Whites rode in front and Blacks rode in back but could sit forward of the rear door when the bus was crowded, if all the Whites had seats. After Lynn paid her fare, she saw that the only seat was in front, but next to a Black lady,[6] so she plopped herself down. She probably said hello and smiled too, because she's that kind of person. The driver suddenly stopped the bus and yelled, "*You!* Stand up *right now!*" Terrified, my sister jumped to her feet. "Not *you*," the driver bellowed, "*her!*" Embarrassed, Lynn said to the lady, "Oh, I'm so sorry!" The lady replied, "Don't worry about it. Just move out into the aisle, so I can get by." Which she did, and they rode the rest of the way in awful silence. It was precisely this kind of insult that moved Blacks to begin the Montgomery bus boycott.

There is a similar story about me that illustrates the confusion and conflicting messages that all Southerners had to deal with. When I was about eight or nine, I was sent to a day camp in Fair Park run by a retired boxer with cauliflower ears, Billy Kramer. He taught me how to swim well. One day at the pool, I wanted a drink of water, but the White drinking fountain was not working (fountains were color coded for the illiterate of both races). I was about to give up and walk away, when a playfellow asked, "Why don't you drink out of the Black one?" "That's for Negroes," I said, using the correct word at the time. "So what?" he asked bluntly. I thought a moment. "Nothing," I said and drank my fill.

I didn't really care who drank out of the fountain, you understand, I just didn't want to get yelled at for breaking the rules. But that little boy, all unknowing, taught me my first lesson in civil disobedience: bugger the rules, especially arbitrary and unjust

---

6. At the time, it was a violation of White manners to refer to African American women as "ladies." Whites always referred to them as "women" and invariably addressed them by their first names only, denying them the title of "Miss" or "Mrs." ("Ms." hadn't been invented yet).

rules. It was an important lesson. I learned that my parents weren't strange; other people in Little Rock did the right thing, too. I grew up to be a Roosevelt Democrat (and I mean Eleanor) and later, a Democratic Socialist on the Canadian and European model (I voted for Sanders twice), and while I owe a lot to my family, I also owe a lot to that commonsensical little boy. "Suffer little children . . . to come unto me" (Matt 19:14). Jesus loves children not just for their innocence but for their honesty.

School, obviously, is one of the most effective institutions in teaching racism to children. When I was in sixth grade (I must have been about twelve), my elementary school, Forest Park, put on a minstrel show, in which the end men (a kind of chorus for the interlocutor, the White master of ceremonies) appeared in blackface and wearing black wigs. I was given the role of reciting the "Psaltre [pronounced p-sal-tree] Sermon" because I had a loud voice that could be heard in the back of the auditorium. I also was dressed in blackface and a nappy black wig.

The sermon portrays a half-educated Black preacher struggling with a sermon that he has not had time to prepare. Every White stereotype of the Black man with little learning is in there ("the text as recorded in two-i Kings," "Moses took his two-bit Barlow knife (the one with the beer opener in the back"). The speech was a great hit (shockingly, it is still available online).

Even my parents thought it was funny and drove me downtown to recite it for Grandaddy Scott (I don't remember whether I was in costume for this). Somebody expressed concern that it might upset his Black nighttime caretaker, but someone else said, "Oh, she's a good sport, she won't mind." Of course the home health aide had no choice in the matter. Suck it up, or be fired. I have an eight-by-ten photograph of me performing at school.

In junior high school, our geography teacher had us write an essay describing an antebellum plantation "big house," as rank a piece of proslavery nostalgia as you can imagine. I had just seen (or maybe read) *Gone with the Wind*, and I remembered the movie *Song of the South*, Walt Disney's perversion of Joel Chandler Harris. Besides, I lived in a house very like that, so I laid it on thick—the tree-lined drive, the porte cochere, the elegant furnishings. I don't remember whether I mentioned slaves or not. I got an A.

Our teachers and principals were holdovers from the Jim Crow era—Edwardians, if you will, or early Wilsonians—with all the racist and imperialist ideals that should have died in the trenches of World War I, but didn't. Those lights of education were still teaching the best and worst of the Western canon, all unaware in 1951 of the cataclysm about to burst over their heads with Brown v. Board of Education of Topeka in 1954.

So, segregation worked like this: Whites said to Blacks, "We'll trust you with our and our children's lives. You can take care of our babies, cook for us (and we trust you not to spit in our soup), and move freely in our homes without stealing more than a little food. But you cannot vote, you must accept starvation wages and daily humiliation, you cannot sit next to us in public transportation or at the movies, you cannot go to school or to the restroom with us. You must allow White men to rape your women, but any attempt at retaliation or what we call miscegenation will be instantly met with the most extreme violence."

Also in junior high school, I took to walking home sometimes instead of taking the bus, and one route took me through West Rock. I wasn't welcome—I saw hard, suspicious looks, though no one ever bothered me. The houses were flimsy board shacks standing on brick piers about eighteen inches or two feet high to raise them above the rainwater that poured down from the hills. My mother told me that one woman was electrocuted when her house flooded and she switched on a light. So, there was no drainage; people just had to wait for the floodwater to evaporate or soak into the ground. It never occurred to me to ask about plumbing, and I was never invited into anyone's home. But when Aunt Ann was remodeling her and Uncle Baldy's bathroom, she offered Julius (who lived in West Rock with his mother) their old bathtub, so there must have been running water.

Across Cantrell Road from West Rock was Riverdale Country Club and Mr. Bullard's grocery and liquor store. Riverdale was sandwiched between the Missouri Pacific tracks to the east and

West Rock to the west, so it was not quite as classy as Little Rock Country Club, which perched on top of the ridge north of us, looking down on the floodplain to the east and the still-forested hills to the north.

Mr. Bullard was the embodiment of the White plantation owner in Henry C. Work's Civil War song "The Year of Jubilo." If he wasn't six feet and three hundred pounds, he was close to it. He kept a few horses in a corral behind his store, and there were always a few men from West Rock hanging around, hoping to pick up an odd job that might earn them a loaf of bread or a quart of wine. "What's the word?" went the radio commercial. "Thunderbird. What's the price? Thirty twice. Tell 'em Jocko sent you."[7]

One day, Mr. Bullard ordered one of the men to saddle and bridle a horse who was a little rowdy. The men all gathered around to watch as two of them hoisted Mr. Bullard into the saddle. As Julius told my father and me, the horse sagged a little at first, then bunched his hooves together and arched his back. Mr. Bullard sailed into the air, and "when he hit the ground, it sounded like a mattress. We all had to run around to the front of the store, so we could laugh."

The discomfiture of the White master is an abiding theme in African American folklore, and here it was in real life.[8] Now that I think of it, it is very revealing that Julius felt comfortable enough with us to tell us about African Americans laughing at Whites at that time.

At different times, Jimmy[9] and Julius both had to deal with a common domestic problem in the South: how to get a possum out of the house in the small hours of the morning. Jimmy and

7. Jocko was the radio announcer. "Thirty twice" means that the wine cost sixty cents a quart.

8. The examples are many, but consider Harris's *Uncle Remus*. Brer Rabbit, the hero, is Black folklore's clever trickster (like Raven or Coyote in Native American tales) who always outwits (and sometimes kills) his more powerful adversary, Brer B'ar, Brer Wolf, etc.—i.e., White Master. I deplore Walt Disney's perversion of the tales in his film *Song of the South* (Jackson, *Song of the South*).

9. My father. We called him Jimmy because our mother did, and our parents thought it was cute.

Mother were awakened by a loud crash in the cellar under their bedroom. Suspecting a burglar, Jimmy grabbed a flashlight and the twelve-gauge shotgun and went outside to the cellar door. It was open, and the flashlight revealed a large possum. Now, a possum is about the size of a large cat and looks like a rat. Armed with formidable teeth and claws, it is popularly supposed to play dead when alarmed, but this one hadn't read the manual and bristled at Jimmy. A lot of guys would have left the cellar door open and gone back to sleep, leaving the possum a way out of the cellar, but some men, once having picked up a loaded gun, have to shoot it. So, Jimmy blazed away, almost directly under Mother's bed. In the confined space, the noise was cataclysmic, and Mother and my siblings screamed in terror (I slept peacefully on the second floor and heard nothing). There was a lot of angry recrimination, not to mention mess. In later years, we laughed heartily at the story and never let Jimmy forget it. Julius, of course, had to clean up.

As Julius was doing so next morning, he told us that once, he had been awakened by a noise in his kitchen in West Rock. Switching on the light, he saw a possum on the table, eating the leftovers. This one didn't play possum either, so Julius let fly with his .410 shotgun. The possum disappeared, replaced by a large hole in the table, Julius's mother shrieked, and the neighbors came running in, expecting a story of theft or maybe even a crime of passion. Everybody had a good laugh, collected the remains of the possum, and cooked and ate it on the spot.

Both Jimmy and Julius used misguided machismo to get rid of their possums, but the reactions of the people around them illustrate the differences of race and class. Julius enjoyed humor and community; Jimmy was left without solace.

Between our hill and Bullard's was a disused rock quarry and a few acres of empty land. During World War II, we used to ride our horses down the hill and across that patch which led to a gravel road along the Arkansas River. Then, my mother and sister would let their horses gallop, while I struggled to urge my balky Shetland pony to a trot. After the war, somebody built an all-White subdivision on the empty land and the quarry and sold the houses to returning GIs and their families. The houses were small, two-bedroom bungalows painted in bright colors. They were typical of the kind of development called Levittowns—after the prototype in New Jersey—going up all over the United States at that time. Twenty years later, Malvina Reynolds would skewer them in her song "Little Boxes." The subdivision was directly across Cantrell Road from West Rock, but the White people in the subdivision could not afford to hire servants, so the bedrock walls of segregation meant that the two ignored each other, while the rich White people on the hills looked down on both the African Americans and the working-class Whites.[10] If a Black person wanted to shop at Bullard's, they had to go to the back door; the front door was reserved for Whites.

I was the third child in my family. My sister, Lynn, is seven years older than I, and my brother, Gordon, was four years older. When Mother was pregnant with me, she hoped she would have twins so I'd have someone to play with, but I was solitary. My parents hired a succession of African American maids to help her cope with us and the constant washing and cleaning that five people made necessary. I had a dim memory of Old Pearl in childhood, but that faded by adolescence. The top of my right ear folds over more than the left, so Mother was fond of recounting that when I was squalling in Old Pearl's arms, she said, "Peter [my middle name], if you ain't good, I'll bite off yo' bad ear." I remembered New Pearl, too, for a while, but that memory faded also in later childhood. After all, New Pearl left when I was only four.

My father was a stockbroker, so his getting married in 1931 in the depths of the Great Depression (when some brokers were throwing themselves out of windows) was a testimony to his courage and ability. Around 1990, there were still people in Arkansas who revered the name of Jimmy Vinson for keeping their parents

10. There is a revealing joke about these racial and class divisions concerning an African American, a poor White man, a rich White man, and a plate of cookies. With a single sentence, the rich White man steals all the cookies, insults and degrades the Black man, and creates a false sense of solidarity with the poor White man, thus deflecting the poor White's anger from the rich White towards the African American.

afloat during the Depression. When World War II came, Jimmy (everyone called him Jimmy, except his mother and aunts, who called him James Russell) tried to enlist, but he was a little too old at thirty-six and had too many children. I don't think that we children made any connection between the war and Jimmy, but Mother must have been very grateful that he was home, because it meant that we had a dad at a time when we desperately needed one. Jimmy closed his brokerage business and went to work in a defense plant near Camp Robinson, a military base on the outskirts of North Little Rock, across the river. The long daily commute meant that he got extra ration coupons for gasoline and tires.[11] Our parents used to pay us a nickel for picking pebbles out of the treads of the tires, but nevertheless, Jimmy's 1940 Ford was beaten almost to death by the end of the war.

American racism is not confined to African Americans. Immediately after Pearl Harbor, President Roosevelt signed Executive Order 9066, which ordered the imprisonment of all persons of Japanese descent, including US citizens. Some of the prisoners were locked up in concentration camps at Rohwer and Jerome, Arkansas, about 150 miles southeast of Little Rock.[12] These prisoners could be released if a White family sponsored them by giving them some menial job (e.g., nanny or gardener) or supported them while they were going to school.[13] Sometime in 1943, then, my parents hired a beautiful Nisei prisoner named Mae Tanabe to be our nanny (Nisei are children born in the US of Japanese

---

11. Rubber and other consumer goods were hard to get during the war, partly because the Japanese had occupied so many of the countries where they came from. The US produced its own gasoline and steel, but they went to the military—new consumer goods just weren't being made.

12. I use the term in its original English sense as used during the Boer War: a place to lock up civilians who have not been charged with a crime for indefinite periods of time (see Oxford Reference, s.v. "concentration camp," https://www.oxfordreference.com/view/10.1093/oi/authority.20110803095630376). Rohwer has almost disappeared; Jerome had a population of thirty-nine in the 2010 census (Wikipedia, s.v. "Jerome, Arkansas," https://en.wikipedia.org/wiki/Jerome,_Arkansas).

13. Thanks to Lynn Tanabe Grannan, daughter of Mae Tanabe and Portland Taiko board co-chair, for the information in this section.

parents). She and her family had been imprisoned in a camp near Rohwer. New Pearl must have left us about this time. I never asked my parents why they hired a Nisei instead of another African American. Most likely, it was because they had a keen sense of right and wrong. Many Americans were dismayed by Roosevelt's injustice, so hiring a Nisei was a way of righting that wrong in our little corner of the world.

Mae lived in a tiny apartment off our garage. Her Nisei husband, Henry, had joined the army before Pearl Harbor. Henry was extremely lucky—many Nisei soldiers were classified as enemy aliens, discharged (despite being US citizens and servicemen), and tossed into concentration camps like Rohwer. Some were allowed to join the 442nd Regimental Combat Team, which covered itself with blood and glory in Europe. But Henry's commander transferred him to a billet at Camp Robinson, near Jimmy's defense plant. That compassion very possibly saved his life. Henry was a technical corporal, a radioman (roughly equivalent to today's specialist), but there was no way an American commander would let a Japanese near a radio, so Henry had very little to do during the war beyond running movie projectors for training films and the like.

Mae and Henry Tanabe during World War II

Mae on her wedding day in the concentration camp at Rohwer, Arkansas

When Henry got a weekend pass, my father took him home on Friday nights so he could spend the weekend with Mae, and Jimmy and he went back to work on Monday morning.

We all loved Mae and Henry. They played with us, and Mae fixed Japanese food. She taught Lynn how to braid her hair (and no doubt fielded her questions about boys), and when I complained to Henry that Gordon was always picking on me, he gave me a couple of lessons in hand-to-hand combat suitable for little boys.

We had a phonograph record of "The Ballad of Casey Jones," the Illinois Central engineer who crashed his train near Vaughan, Mississippi. I used to line up all the dining-room chairs and have Mae put on the record. When the verse came that says, "Now the caller called Casey 'bout half-past four / He kissed his wife at the station door / He mounted to the cabin with his orders in his hand . . . ,"[14] I would kiss Mae and clamber into the lead chair to start my fatal ride. I made her do this over and over. I understand now that Mother was so preoccupied with caring for my brother that I was starved for sheer physical comfort, which Mae lovingly provided.

Around the time that Mae arrived, my brother Gordon was stricken with polio, which paralyzed his left leg. He was nine years

14. "Casey Jones."

old. I remember almost nothing of this, but my sister, Lynn, and Mae's daughter (whom she named after my sister) have told me about those grim days. My sister says that he was deathly ill at home for a week before he could be moved to a hospital, and Lynn Tanabe says that he was in an iron lung. It was good that we had the twin blessings of Mae Tanabe and a father too old (and too prolific) for the army! Mother was completely consumed with Gordon's care, snatching him off to Warm Springs, Georgia, where President Roosevelt was treated for the same illness, researching doctors and therapists and treatment. Mae became a mother to me, a big sister to Lynn, and a cook and housekeeper to all of us.

In a triumph of youthful confidence, Mae got pregnant toward the end of the war (when Roosevelt's order was lifted) and bore a daughter, whom she named Lynn, after my sister. I can't remember if she was still working for us, but when Henry was discharged at the end of the war, they moved to Michigan and farmed. They had a son, Robert, and settled down to rebuilding their lives in postwar America. My mother and sister kept in touch with Mae and Henry and, after their deaths, with her daughter, Lynn.

I did not keep in touch. For one thing, I was only six when the war ended and didn't know how to write. But even after I learned, I didn't want to write. I told myself that I had been a baby, and I didn't like being reminded of my babyish ways. Decades later, I came to understand a deeper reason.

In our sixties, my sister, Lynn, and I spent a lot of time dissecting our childhood and family. She summed it up in one succinct sentence: "Before Gordon got sick, everything was pretty much okay. But once he got sick, everything went to hell."

Mother was distraught, devastated, unable to cope. Any parent would be grief-stricken, but Mother was obsessed with making Gordon whole. Decades later, when I was piecing together the family history, I telephoned her to ask when Gordon had been stricken. Without missing a beat at the unexpected question, she said briskly, "1943, and it broke your grandfather's heart." Grandaddy? How did he get into this? I was too stunned to ask, "What about Gordon's heart? What about yours?" After the call, reflecting on what I knew about her relationship with her mother (who had died before Gordon got sick), I reckoned that Mother had been conditioned as a child to be perfect for her parents, and, having decided to be a mother and distinguished matron, she had to have a perfect family. Therefore, Gordon's being crippled by polio reflected badly on her; in her own mind, she had let her parents down by allowing that to happen to her child.

There was a lot of stigma against the handicapped then, and Gordon never recovered from it. He suffered greatly in the outside world. He grew to be a handsome, brilliant man, strong and well proportioned, but a late-stage alcoholic by the time he was in college, and it killed him at thirty-three. Only as I write does it occur to me that his bullying of me was a reaction to the bullying and teasing that he suffered at school every day.

Lynn and I effectively lost our mother at critical junctures in our lives—Lynn as she entered adolescence, and I in infancy. Mae filled that void for both of us, and while Lynn managed Mae's departure with some degree of aplomb, I lost a second mother. I don't remember feeling angry at Mae for leaving but rather a deep sense of hurt and loss that I did not know how to express. The absence of a mother, compounded by bullying from my siblings and medicated with alcohol from late adolescence until I was forty, plagued me and ruined my relationships with others for many years.

Sometime after sobering up, I telephoned Mae and wrote to her, thanking her for her love and care and apologizing for not having kept in touch. She kept my letter and showed it to her Lynn. My Lynn and I managed to meet her son, Bob, when we all happened to be in Arizona, and then in 2016, my wife and I traveled to Oregon to meet Lynn and her husband. The next year, Lynn Tanabe (her maiden name) went to Portland, Maine, to meet Lynn Vinson, and the circle was closed. If I have not paid, I have at least acknowledged my debt.

In 1997 (long before I met the adult Tanabe children), I took a trip through Arkansas, Mississippi, and Tennessee to search out the homes of our ancestors. While on the way to Hamburg,

Arkansas (where a great-grandfather enlisted for the Civil War), I suddenly saw an inscribed white obelisk at the entrance to a farm.

Obelisk erected by former prisoners in the camp at Jerome, Arkansas

I stopped and backed up, and there was a monument to the Jerome Relocation Center, a concentration camp not far from Rohwer. I placed a stone on the pedestal, and as I took pictures, the farmer appeared. He was about my age. We shared our stories. He told me that he and his brother had played with the Nisei children and later donated the land for the obelisk. "They were fine people," he said. Indeed, they were. The anti-Asian racist violence shown by Trump and his followers enrages me.

So, by the time I was six, when the war ended, I knew about racism and injustice, and knew that my government (which public school was teaching me to admire) could be guilty of them. I knew nothing of my own racism, but I would find out.

One day when I was eight or nine, Gordon had been bullying me (I don't remember what it was about, but it could be pretty serious). I was hurt and angry, but I knew it was wrong to hit a disabled person, so I stuffed it. When I met Julius shortly after, I said something ugly to him. I have no memory of what I said, but it was a piece of racism calculated to hurt him and make him feel small. He could not say or do anything, of course, just as I had had to swallow the hurt from my brother. A few hours later that day, I wanted to go somewhere on my bike. This was not a matter of just getting on the bike and going; the road on our woodlot went downhill and east, and I wanted to go uphill and west, which meant pushing the bike uphill through the woods until I reached the paved road through the neighborhood to the west, behind us. That was a heavy job for a small boy, so I asked Julius to carry or push the bike for me. He did so without question, and then he kindly, patiently explained that he was glad to help me, but that what I had said to him a little before had hurt him badly and he had done nothing to deserve it. I hope that I apologized—I hope that I thanked him for helping me—but I have absolutely no memory of what I said or did. Almost eighty years later, the memory of this incident shrivels me with shame.

We sometimes hired Julius to wait at table at family holiday dinners. With the five of us, plus Aunt Anne and Uncle Baldy, Great-Aunts Blanche and Ruth, Grandmother Vinson, and Grandaddy Scott, plus the odd cousin or three, we might be fourteen people, so help was needed. It was like living in Downton Abbey. The cooking alone took several days; the table settings lacked a device to measure the placement, but we had the full silver service, including individual salt cellars and tiny silver spoons to go with them.

As the years went by, Julius sank deeper into alcoholism and became unreliable, often getting arrested for drunkenness. He knew our habits, so he timed his call from the jail for the middle of Thanksgiving or Christmas dinner, when I was assigned to answer the phone—he knew that I would be sympathetic and would convey his message to Jimmy to come down and bail him out. Jimmy always swore quietly and went, driving miles to the isolated, gray, four-story city lockup on East Markham to get him out and take him home to West Rock. These messages became so frequent that I was finally told to tell Julius that Jimmy couldn't come.

Yet, when Grandmother Vinson fell at age ninety and broke her hip (the only time she was ever sick that I can remember), it was Julius who found her, picked her up, put her to bed, and made the necessary phone calls. Thank you, Julius.

My mother sometimes had to defend one of the maids. Once, a stock boy at our grocery store called our maid Bessie the N-word. Mother got on the phone and gave the owner hark from the tomb, telling him that she expected her employees to receive the same respectful treatment that she got, and that if anything like that happened again, she would take her business elsewhere and advise her friends to do so, too. As mother knew a lot of well-to-do matrons among the store's customers, this was no idle threat. We had no more trouble.

The code was that if a Black person worked for you, he or she was "your help" (to use a euphemism), and both White authorities and the Black community expected you to take care of him or her. It was a little survival of antebellum ways.

In the South in the 1940s, the Civil War was not far away. Really, the United States can never come to terms with its racism until it admits that the South won the war with Union help. Yes, the Confederate army was destroyed. Yes, the Confederate government was dissolved and many leaders were jailed. But the Union allowed the social and economic systems of the South to remain unchanged for the next hundred years. Reconstruction (1863–77) failed because no significant number of Northern leaders believed that freed slaves were capable of becoming citizens.[15] Within a couple of years after Union troops left the South in 1877, all the gains that Blacks had made since emancipation (schools, members of congress and state legislatures—all that) were erased by the same old Southern White power structure and the Ku Klux Klan. The federal government did nothing to protect Black progress.

True, the United States passed the Civil Rights Act in 1964 and the Voting Rights Act in 1965, a century after the war, but then the United States Supreme Court gutted the Voting Rights Act in Shelby County v. Holder in 2013. America can take strong action for a short time but is unwilling to make the sustained effort required to eliminate racism.

15. On the question of Black suffrage, see Foner, *Reconstruction* (throughout).

After the Civil War, slavery was replaced by debt peonage in the form of sharecropping—and not just for Blacks but for Whites as well. There were many different agreements between the plantation owner and the sharecropper, but at bottom, the former lent or gave the latter—maybe on a rent-to-own basis—seed, tools, a mule, or any or all of those in return for a share of the crop, which the sharecropper labored to plant, cultivate, and harvest. If the crop failed, then the debt carried over to the next year (with interest, of course). In addition, the sharecropper could buy tools, parts, and food staples at the plantation's store, which had the advantage of being much closer than the store in town but the disadvantage of being more expensive. Here, too, debt rolled over from one bad year to the next (with interest, of course), landing the sharecropper, Black or White, in an unending cycle of labor and poverty.

My maternal grandfather, Sterling Price Scott, the son of a Confederate veteran (of whom more later), was an accountant on a plantation owned by a man named Thompson.

My grandfather Sterling Price Scott

As a young man (ca. 1890 or so), Grandaddy kept the books at the company store (set up because town was too far away) and knew all about maintaining constant debt. People of both races did the same labor in adjacent, identical fields, shopped at the same store, and endured the same cycle of poverty and scanty education.[16]

The poor White identified, and identifies today, with the rich White because his race is the only thing he can cling to which makes him (in his own eyes) a little bit better than the person of color. Whiteness gives him a little bit of hope that maybe his children or grandchildren won't have to pick cotton or—its twenty-first century equivalent—shift boxes at Amazon.

The rich White (my ancestors among them, as I explain in chapter 6) has fostered this race/class division since the seventeenth century, because he can use it to keep the poor of both races in their place.[17] America is doomed to keep its racism until we cease this division between rich and poor.

There was another way in which Grandaddy exemplified the post-Reconstruction South. In his teens (say, about 1880), he and a Black companion got a job laying track for the Missouri-Pacific Railroad. They each had a mule and each got a dollar a day for this backbreaking labor, out of which they had to feed the mules. They slept where the track ended at night and turned to after breakfast next morning. Mother told me this story after Grandaddy's death and knew no other details. But Grandaddy was White and had enough schooling to become an accountant, while his Black companion did not.

When I was a little boy, my mother took me to visit old ladies who had been her mother's friends. They let me play with the .44 Army Colt revolvers that their fathers had carried in the Civil War. Once, we sat under the oil portrait of a Confederate captain[18] who,

16. See, for example, Ashmore, *Epitaph for Dixie*, 12, 13: "I poured Aleck [Miss Betty's Black handyman] a drink of whiskey. I poured it, by certain instinct, in the special glass, the jelly glass, set apart from the others." Ashmore thus makes it clear that even genteel, Vassar College-educated White ladies (like my mother) maintained this barrier. For the generational effects of this system, see Maharidge and Williamson, *And Their Children*.

17. Isenberg, *White Trash*, esp. chaps. 1–7.

18. Captain John Gould Fletcher. To see a photo of Captain Fletcher, see

in 1958, glared down at his daughter and her friends as they plotted to integrate the public schools of Little Rock. Grandmother Vinson always referred to the "Great Emancipator" as "that old Lincoln," and when Great-Aunt Ruth visited Cousin Fred in Washington, he loaned her his limousine with strict instructions to the Black chauffeur to show her Washington but not to let her catch sight of the Lincoln Memorial.[19]

Her sister-in-law's outlook on race was more flexible. Many years later, my parents sold the house on the hill and moved into a high-rise, but they kept up the tradition of family dinners. One Christmas, my father drove downtown to get Great-Aunt Blanche and his mother (now both almost ninety), and when they came into the high-rise apartment, it was clear that Jimmy was suppressing laughter with some difficulty. He explained later that when they had gotten into the self-operated elevator, Grandmother had snorted, "Hmff. I'd rather have a n— over there running it for us." To which Aunt Blanche retorted, "Well, if you talk like that, you can't be much of a segregationist, can you?"

When Great-Aunt Blanche came to visit at Thanksgiving and Christmas, she always told us Papa's story. Papa was my great-grandfather, First Lieutenant Exum Vinson, CSA.[20]

Papa had been wounded and captured at Silver Spring, Maryland, an event Great-Aunt Blanche referred to as "when Papa had his accident," the accident being a random (but quite purposeful) .58-caliber Minié ball through his shin. He lay on the field for a

Roberts and Moneyhon, *Portraits of Conflict*, 31. For information about his life, see Roberts and Moneyhon, *Portraits of Conflict*, 219.

19. "Cousin" Fred Vinson was chief justice of the Supreme Court under President Franklin Roosevelt. In the midst of World War II, when train travel was strictly limited, Great-Aunt Ruth, using my father's name, called Senator Fulbright's office, got a rare berth in a Pullman car to Washington, and scraped an acquaintance with Cousin Fred on the pretext that her father and his father had both been born in Northampton County, North Carolina, so we had to be kin. None of us took her seriously, but perhaps we should have; Vinsons are thick upon the ground in Northampton County. My father was deeply embarrassed.

20. One of his sons, Joseph Exum, was the second of that name; Ekky (his grandson's nickname) was the third.

day and a night before a Yankee ambulance picked him up. Papa had the presence of mind to hide his pistol in his boot, but pulled it out and threatened to shoot the Yankee surgeon who wanted to amputate. He kept his leg, but not the pistol. I learned later that he had been an illiterate plowboy when he joined the army but taught himself to read and write in his spare time and rose to company commander.

Later, the Yankees tried to recruit this nettlesome prisoner to go out West and shoot Native Americans, but Exum was loyal till the last. Reasoning that he cost his captors more as a prisoner than he would as a galvanized Yankee, he declared, "I told you and I told you: no, God damn you, no!" When the war ended, Exum and other loyal Confederates refused to go home, because the Ironclad Oath (an oath of loyalty to the United States) included the phrase "I take this obligation freely, without any mental reservation or purpose of evasion."[21] None of this was true, so the prisoners refused to sign. Since the Yankees wanted to go home, too, and since the prisoners were costing them a lot of money, the Yankees had to give in and strike the offending clause.

At home in North Carolina, Exum hung around for a while, married Great-Grandmother Molly, sired my grandfather Baldy Sr. (named after an army buddy), packed them into a wagon, and moved to Augusta, Arkansas, where he opened a store and joined the Ku Klux Klan. When the Yankees came looking for him at dawn one morning, Molly, in wrapper and curl papers, held them off and stalled for time while she dressed before she let them search the house.

21. Wikipedia, s.v. "Ironclad Oath," https://en.wikipedia.org/wiki/Ironclad_Oath.

**My great-grandparents Exum and Molly with their children
(back row: Grandfather Baldy Sr., Great-Uncle Russ;
front row: Great-Aunts Blanche and Ruth)**

So, I grew up with this legend of endurance, resistance, and deep suspicion of authority, witnessing the abuse of African Americans and Asian Americans by my race and learning of the defeat and military occupation of my own people. I was divided, like most Southerners of my generation. On the one hand, Exum was a hero, thwarting the enemy and occupying army at every turn. On the other hand, I loved Mae and Julius, and my parents had taught me that Blacks were the equals of Whites in every way, that segregation was unjust, that the Klan was a vicious, cowardly organization. It took me many years to put all of that together.

The dueling concepts that my great-grandfather had been a brave Confederate soldier (I did not yet know that two other ancestors had fought for the Confederacy, let alone that they were slave owners) but that he had fought for slavery and injustice against freedom and democracy and had become a Klansman were impossible to reconcile. How could I claim my family without denying justice? How could I proclaim justice without denying my family? My dad dealt with the problem by accepting his ancestors' courage and endurance and by becoming a crack shot, like his father, aunt, and grandfather. If he saw the ancestors in conflict with justice, he probably didn't frame it to himself in those words; they were simply different men in a different era. I was close to my dad, but we never discussed this; like him, I simply accepted the ancestors as they were, without feeling bound by them. My sister and brother thought Great-Aunt Blanche and her stories were boring and silly. They and my mother laughed at Great-Grandfather's name, Exum, thinking it backward and countrified (I found out decades later that it is a surname, fairly common in North Carolina and Kentucky). The three of them felt, I believe, that nothing good could come out of Arkansas or the South of that time. So, given the opportunity to escape to prep schools and colleges in New England, with concomitant access to the cultural riches of New York, they leapt at it and rejected their heritage without hesitation.

To a large extent, I did the same as my siblings and mother for a long time. The world outside of Arkansas was fascinating, rich, and varied, so I was eager to make my way in it. But in the end, my siblings became the galvanized Yankees, and I ended up in Arizona, in many important respects so like the Arkansas of the 1950s: bigoted, poor, and badly educated.[22] Here, too, we murmur a sigh of relief and whisper, "Thank God for Mississippi!" Poor Mississippi always ranked forty-seventh or forty-eighth (we had only forty-eight states until 1959) by most measures when I was a boy, and remains forty-ninth or fiftieth today, when not displaced by Arizona. But I remembered the old stories and was fascinated by them.

22. Estimates vary but consistently place Arizona at thirty-ninth, forty-fifth, or forty-seventh in the nation in education. It was ranked forty-ninth in education in 2021 according to WalletHub (Rivera, "Third-Worst School System"). Cathy Hoffman, Arizona's bravely outspoken superintendent of public instruction, says, "Our Legislature has failed to even fund all-day kindergarten, let alone preschool of any kind. . . . [M]any Arizona children, disproportionately low-income children and children of color, do not have access to preschool at all. . . . [O]nly 16% of 3- and 4-year-olds in our state are enrolled in publicly funded preschool. This means that the majority of kids are starting kindergarten already behind their peers through no fault of their own" (Hoffman, "AZ Schools," paras. 5–6).

Chapter 3

The Little Rock School Crisis
and the Wider World

I N 1954 (the year the US Supreme Court decided Brown v. Board of Education), I was sent to what was then called a "progressive" boarding school, the Putney School in southern Vermont.

The school was diverse, not only racially but politically. The Latin teacher was a German Jew who married the Italian woman who had hidden him during Fascism. The art teacher was a Spaniard who had fought on the Republican side during the Spanish Civil War and married a Russian. One of the English teachers, Jeff Campbell, was an African American who was married to a White woman and had run for governor of Massachusetts on the Socialist ticket. I knew Yankees did things like that, so I didn't let it bother me; in fact, I often turned to Jeff for advice, even after I went to college. There were several students of different races there, among them a boy from Tonga, a Black boy from Arkansas, and a Black girl from Philadelphia.[1] Today, Putney's philosophy and practices are old hat, because so many alumni grew up to found their own progressive schools around the country. But in the '50s, in the McCarthy era, Putney was considered radical and left wing and had a public relations problem, particularly with its conservative Yankee

1. Through the metamorphosis of time, she has become a prominent educator and writer. How was I to know?

neighbors. The students of different races had different schedules than I and were of different ages, so I had little contact with them.

Besides, to be honest, I was reclusive and had trouble adapting to Putney or, indeed, to any group that I might fall into. As an aging adult, my friends call me eccentric and my wife's friends tell her that I am autistic. A psychiatrist once said to me, years after he had treated me, "I've had thousands of patients, Sterling, but you were . . ." He broke off, and I imagine that he had been about to say, "a real mess." But perhaps not. In any case, social situations are hard for me. I do not "fit in." At some point, I can be counted on to say exactly the wrong thing to the wrong person.

The summer before I entered Putney, I was sent to its summer camp. On an overnight hiking trip, something said around the campfire triggered an association in my mind, and without thinking, I started a racist limerick. I had forgotten that one of the other children was an African American girl, and halfway through, I realized what an awful thing I was saying. I stopped cold in shame, but she just giggled and said, "Oh, I don't mind, go ahead." It's another of those memories that makes my flesh crawl seventy years later. Partial redemption came a year or so later, when a train was taking carloads of preppies to New York before we dispersed for some long vacation. The Black girl from Philadelphia was getting unwanted attention from a Black boy (not from Putney), so she asked me to sit with her and chat to get rid of him. I did so, and now at eighty-two I feel good about the trust she showed me.

There was, of course, a lot of discussion at Putney about Brown v. Board of Education when it came down. The case is of monumental importance in American race law, because it reverses Plessy v. Ferguson (handed down in 1896). The latter case had established the pernicious doctrine of "separate but equal" in nationwide law and practice, enshrining segregation of the races and, in effect, endorsing what the Ku Klux Klan had long struggled for, the barring of African Americans from all but the most menial positions in society, especially in White society. I remember one boy asking a teacher why, if facilities were equal, Blacks should object to being separate. The teacher and I were hard put to explain that separation itself implies inferiority, because we had never before had to put such an idea into words. It was a new thought in American life, and our struggle to express it mirrored in a small way what the justices had gone through to reach their unanimous decision.

In September of 1957, I was on my way to enter Harvard when I heard on the radio that Governor Orval Faubus of Arkansas had called out the National Guard to prevent the integration of Little Rock's public schools. It was a shocking development; the governor was defying federal law as expressed in Brown v. Board of Education. It was puzzling as well, because as governor, Faubus had presided over the integration of other school districts around the state without a fuss. The reason, I believed then and believe still, was that Faubus wanted another term as governor, and a show of independence would almost guarantee his reelection. Republican General Eisenhower was president, so a Democratic governor with enough sand to stand up to the federals, especially to the general who had conquered Hitler's *Wehrmacht*, was sure to be a hero.

Which is what happened. Eisenhower dithered for a few days, then nationalized the Arkansas Guard, sent them home, and sent two battalions of US Army paratroopers from Fort Bragg to escort nine heroic Black children into high school. Faubus cannily waited until the end of the school year, when the paratroopers went back to their base. Then he closed the public schools, and Eisenhower was stymied. Both were reelected in November.

In 1958, the women took over. The leader was Mrs. Adolphine Fletcher Terry, seventy years old and daughter of a Confederate captain. She had been instrumental in starting progressive changes in Little Rock for many years. Among these was good treatment of the handicapped. One of her daughters, Mary, had cerebral palsy, which confined her to a wheelchair. There was a great deal of ignorance about and prejudice against the handicapped at the time, especially against people with cerebral palsy, who were popularly believed to be mentally deficient. Nevertheless, Mary and her activist mother courageously appeared at the Robinson Auditorium for every performance of the Little Rock Symphony Orchestra (which Mrs. Terry had founded).

Mrs. Terry was stung into action against segregation by a letter from an old friend, Mrs. Velma Powell, demanding to know why Mrs. Terry had not used her considerable influence to help reopen the schools. Mrs. Terry responded by inviting Powell and a close mutual friend of our family, Vivion Brewer, to an organizational meeting at her home. There in her parlor, with Captain Fletcher's portrait glaring down from the wall, the three women put together a list of Little Rock matrons (including my mother, Louise Scott Vinson). These women pressured the menfolk to open the schools by pointing out to them, insistently, that closed schools would do a lot of economic damage to Arkansas. The businesses and industries that the men wanted to attract would not come to a state that had no public schools.

The women's group adopted the catchy title of the Women's Emergency Committee to Open Our Schools, quickly shortened to the WEC. The group immediately came into conflict with the Black community, headed by Daisy Bates, president of the Arkansas branch of the National Association for the Advancement of Colored People. All over the country, both Blacks and progressive Whites, outraged by injustice, were fighting for control of the just-born civil rights movement, and the strains of racism showed up here, too.

Nationally, the Whites wanted to be in charge, because they always had been, arguing that they had the connections and influence. Blacks wanted to be in charge, because it was their fight and freedom meant that they should control their own destiny. Their leaders had forged the same connections, and they were going to get the same influence or know the reason why.

In Little Rock, the national media gave more coverage to the Blacks, at least in part because of the novelty of Black leadership, and because Daisy Bates was a powerful young dynamo compared to Adolphine Terry, Vivion Brewer, and Louise Vinson, Southern ladies who had been trained all their lives to be "ladylike" and to take a back seat to White men.

But what really crippled the WEC was its own unconscious bias. When Daisy Bates (later, Dr. Bates) offered to join, bringing with her other Black female leaders, the WEC rejected them. Vivion Brewer (not seeing her own contradictory stance) later wrote, "To combat the hysterical foes of integration we must defeat them and their proposals at the polls" (i.e., by preventing Faubus's reelection). "To amass a vote assuring such defeat . . . we must not, in any way, give any basis for the . . . accusation that we were integrationists. Over and over we proclaimed: 'We stand neither for integration nor for segregation but for education.' It would be suicide to accept Negro women as members. It would be fatal to be seen at a meeting of Negroes. It was dangerous to visit the Arkansas Council on Human Relations[2] . . . Our sharpest weapon was the vote. The integrationist vote was a feeble minority. The Negro vote was small and uninformed. If we accepted or tolerated a single hint of favoring integration, we were a lost cause."[3]

For Vivion, "suicide," "fatal," and "dangerous" was uncharacteristicly strong language, and Dr. Bates must have been infuriated by "feeble" and "uninformed." The issue of integration/civil rights raised and continues to raise uncomfortable levels of subconscious tension in White people.

Of course, everyone knew that opening the schools at all would mean integration, because that was the law. So, the WEC's refusal to accept Black members just made the former look racist and indecisive and compromised the value of their work. They were charming, gracious Southern ladies of the Victorian and Edwardian eras (Mrs. Terry was born in 1888, Vivion Brewer in 1900, my mother in 1907) who did their best to deal with the enormous changes they faced. It was as if Melanie Wilkes and Scarlet O'Hara had decided to cooperate with Rev. Dr. William Barbour II. Nothing in their lives had prepared them for such upheavals in American life. It is no wonder that they blundered; it is remarkable

---

2. An integrated group.

3. Brewer, *Embattled Ladies*, 70–71. Vivion did not write her book until 1972. Her niece, Patricia Murphey Rostker, is probably who sent it to the publisher. Full disclosure: the Brewers were close personal friends of ours, and I named my oldest daughter after Vivion. She has been relentless in rooting out Dad's biases.

that women of their age and background in that place and time made the effort that they did.

In the end, the public schools did open in 1959. But it was a Pyrrhic victory, because by that time segregationist entrepreneurs had begun to open private, or "Christian," academies. As private schools that did not accept government money, they could exclude Blacks, New Yorkers, Muslims, or anyone else they wanted to, just as charter schools (which do take government money) do today, ignoring the teachings of Jesus that all are welcome.

Vivion Brewer and her husband, Joe, paid a high price for supporting integration. Joe had a fairly high civil service rank-ing as a personnel officer in the Veterans Administration, but his Arkansas boss fired him shortly before he retired, so he lost his pension. Joe sued, but got nowhere, and he was a broken man after that.

Governor Faubus had no idea that he was helping to destroy public education in America—he just wanted to get reelected in Arkansas. And he did—he stayed in the governor's office, winning election after election, until 1967, when he retired to open a theme park called Dogpatch, a self-parody of hillbilly life. Someone once asked a former governor, Sid McMath, what had been his biggest mistake. He replied that his mistake was making Orval Faubus state road commissioner so that he could come out of Madison County (the last county in Arkansas to get electricity).[4] Arkansans are good at self-parody; it's our way of laughing at outsiders who laugh at us.[5]

It is worth expanding on self-parody, because it was a device used not only in African American folklore but also by real-life African Americans to deflect or minimize White anger and turn it into indulgent humor.

The name Dogpatch came from a mythical village in a comic strip called *Li'l Abner* by Al Capp about a family of hillbillies named

---

4. Ashmore, *Arkansas*, 152.

5. For the school crisis, I am indebted to Dr. Elizabeth Jacoway, younger sister of my school friend Bronson Jacoway. Her book *Turn Away Thy Son* is invaluable.

Yokum living somewhere in the South. Li'l Abner was a muscular, handsome (for a comic strip) but rather dim guy; his girlfriend was a skimpily clad blonde named Daisy Mae, who was always about to bust out of her blue jean cutoffs and gingham blouse (a Dolly Parton avant la lettre). The Yokums lived in a log cabin with a tilting chimney. Their friends made moonshine.[6] Everyone wore ragged clothes (especially Daisy Mae), and though I read the strip daily for years in my childhood, I cannot remember a single plot. Mammy Yokum did get off one memorable line, "Good is better than evil because it's nicer," which pretty much sums up the problem of life. Orval Faubus should have taken it to heart.

Arkansas has been a target for this kind of parody for about two hundred years. The original lithographs of the story of the "Arkansas Traveler" date at least as early as the 1840s, to judge from the style of the traveler's clothes. The story and song portray a native sitting on the porch of his leaky cabin during a rainstorm and playing the first half of the tune on his fiddle. An out-of-stater comes along, and the two enter a dialogue of jokes that were old when Jonah gagged the whale. The idea was that the reader of *Harper's Weekly* or some similar magazine would laugh at the native, but to the Arkansas reader, the joke is on the traveler.

So with Arkansas ethnic jokes. They are unquestionably the worst I have ever heard. Incest is a frequent topic, bestiality less so, and necrophilia rare but not unheard of, more or less in the order that hillbillies in general and Arkansans in particular are popularly imagined to indulge in them.[7] These jokes are carried to the point of farce so that the point is against the listener foolish enough to believe that Arkansans commit these sins more than other people.

As with Whites, so with Blacks. Southern Whites (and a lot of Northerners, too) imagined African Americans, especially slaves, to be not just uneducated but unintelligent, scared of "hants" and "ghosteses," incapable of managing their own affairs. Blacks knew this, of course, and it often suited their purposes to have Whites

6. One was a parody of a Native American named Lonesome Polecat, as offensive a piece of racism as you could find.

7. See Randolph, *Pissing in the Snow*, 11, 18, 44, 47, 80.

believe in their childish naiveté. I recall two news items from the *Arkansas Gazette*. In one, a Black man charged with assault appeared before a judge, who asked him what he had to say for himself. The man replied, "Fightin's not so bad when it's with kinfolks, judge."

"What relation is this man to you?"

"He's my husband in law."

After restoring order, the judge told the plaintiff to explain. He replied, "He's my girl friend's husband. That makes him my husband in law." The judge fined him twenty-five dollars. That was pretty stiff for a Black man in those days, but much better than ninety days on the county farm.

The second story starts with the air controller at Adams Field (not yet designated an airport) noticing a column of smoke rising every day from the swamps east of the field, always from the same place. In winter, he dismissed it simply as someone's cabin, but when the smoke persisted into midsummer, he got suspicious and called the sheriff, Tom Gulley. After all, who keeps a fire going all day in July in Arkansas? The *Arkansas Gazette* sent along a reporter and photographer, and they all came upon a good-sized still operated by a cheerful Black man named Napoleon Cox.

Instead of resisting or running (which would have gotten him killed), Mr. Cox played innocent, unconscious of any wrong. He cheerfully showed the White gentlemen around, explained how the still worked, and posed smiling for the camera. He admitted that sometimes rats fell into the mash tuns, but said it didn't matter, since the distilling process sterilized the brew.[8]

I never found out what happened to Mr. Cox, but it is clear that he was no naïf. He was a hardworking entrepreneur with a sizable physical plant which had been in operation for many months, and he was smart enough to know that if you play dumb and make people laugh when you're in trouble, your punishment will likely be less severe. He just forgot why we call his product moonshine.[9]

8. These two stories appeared in the *Arkansas Gazette*. I am writing them from memory, as they are from many years ago.

9. My great-uncle Joe (Exum's baby brother) was a revenuer—that is, an

In both cases, the men played up to the White stereotype of the Black man and used it to their advantage.

I was frustrated at Harvard. I wanted to be in Little Rock at a time like that, doing . . . I'm not sure what. My parents mailed me all the newspaper clippings about the schools. I wrote letters to the *Arkansas Gazette*, which they published, because the editor, Harry Ashmore, was a friend of my parents. But I wanted to be there, in the action. I wanted to take part in the Freedom Rides, to join other students who were traveling south to register Black voters, but I had no idea how to go about it. Where should I go? Whom should I contact? And, to be honest, I really didn't want to get beaten up or set on fire. It never occurred to me to turn to the faculty of Harvard for advice. I never thought of asking the college for a leave of absence, and anyway, I feared that my parents would object. They were sticklers for the rules, and something so unorthodox would worry them.

Had I but known, the answer was literally at my doorstep in the form of John Usher Monro, dean of the college. We both lived in Adams House (one of the fancy dormitories for upperclassmen), and we occasionally passed each other in the foyer, but I never thought of talking to him. In 1967, Dean Monro left Harvard to teach at Miles College, a historically Black school near Birmingham, Alabama. After ten years at Miles, he moved to Tougaloo, another historically Black college, where he taught for another twenty years. But all of that was in the future, and as far as I knew, he was just the dean. He would have been the ideal advisor, but I knew nothing about his years of work to integrate Harvard, so I had no reason to approach him, nothing (I thought) to talk to him about. So, my chance was wasted.

While at Putney and Harvard, I was close friends with a young man, John, from New York, who often invited me to spend short holidays (like Thanksgiving or Easter weekends) with him and his family in their apartment on the Upper West Side. John's stepmother was an attorney, and his father edited a magazine. One

---

agent for what was then called the Bureau of Alcohol and Tobacco, tasked with the dangerous job of catching moonshiners.

evening, we attended a soirée at which Dr. Martin Luther King Jr. and some of his aides were present, while a Black musician (could it have been Oscar Brown?) presented the outline of a musical that he hoped Dr. King would endorse. Following that, the conversation moved generally to a discussion of civil rights issues, and I had the temerity to ask Dr. King a question much discussed on campus: whether White students' participation in the Freedom Rides and voter-registration drives was meaningful to the Black participants. Dr. King assured me that it was. Sixty years later, I am astounded to think that I did not ask him there and then how to get involved. It simply didn't occur to me. I had always been taught that I wasn't supposed to bother adults, let alone important adults, with my childish concerns, so I kept my mouth shut with the one man who could have best solved my problem.

While I was at college, my father accidentally took part in a sit-in. My parents were very private people (my mother had written to tell me that my letters to the *Gazette* might hurt my father's business), and my father was especially shy, even withdrawn. Activism just wasn't their thing. One day, Jimmy left his office when the stock market closed in New York and went downstairs for his customary coffee break at Walgreens. In those days, drugstores existed independently of grocery and variety stores and had soda fountains where you could sit at a counter and get a soda or coffee, and even pie or a hamburger. Jimmy vaguely sensed that there weren't many customers that day but, engrossed in his newspaper, didn't even see the half dozen or so Black students with their homework at the other end of the counter. After a while, he realized that he hadn't been served yet, so he looked up to see what was going on. There were the students at one end of the counter and the White waitresses and cashier at the other, the Whites glaring at him.

A cop detached himself from the other Whites and sauntered casually past Jimmy, the way good ole boys do when they want to start trouble. As he passed my father, he murmured, "You son of a bitch," thinking that Jimmy was part of the sit-in.

Jimmy had been about to leave, but the insult made him mad, so he stayed put and read about cotton futures in the *Memphis Commercial Appeal* until the manager said to him, "Mr. Vinson, I'm really afraid there's going to be trouble." Jimmy was supporting three fledgling children and really wasn't prepared to go to jail that afternoon, so he left.

To be fair to my parents, I must say that they did a great deal for integration (as we called civil rights then) in their quiet way. In addition to her work on the WEC, my mother served on the board of the Urban League for a long time, and they gave generously to Philander Smith College, the local, historically Black college (now fully accredited and thriving). But my father was a stockbroker, and while our immediate social circle was made up of intelligent, well-educated people, many of his customers were small businessmen steeped in the customs of the old ways, so he had to be discreet. Besides that, they raised three children to be, if not free of racism, at least free of racial hatred in a society steeped in violent prejudice.

Decades later, I asked my mother how she and my father had freed themselves from racial prejudice. She gave a kind of sighing laugh, and said, "Oh, I don't know that we ever did, really." They were both educated at Ivy League schools (very unusual at the time) and that certainly had a lot to do with it, but they were really just quiet, decent people who hated violence and injustice, especially when founded on ignorance and fear.

When I graduated from college in 1961, I was faced with the same problem as every other American male: what to do about military service. The possibilities were to go to graduate school (and hope the army would have forgotten you by the time you got out), be drafted into the army for two years, or enlist. I could not face reading professional books for another four years, so I decided to enlist in the Navy's Officer Candidate School. This meant three years of active duty instead of two, but as an officer, I would have enough money to marry my girlfriend, so I did that.

I went through Officer Candidate School (near the bottom of my class) at Newport, RI. There was one Issei (third-generation

Japanese American) in my company, but I do not remember any African Americans in my class. While serving as legal officer on a ship, I heard unofficially about an interracial brawl among some enlisted men—some Whites insulted some Blacks, and the latter swabbed the deck with the former. Filipinos at that time could only serve as stewards—i.e., officers' servants.

Eventually, I ended up on shore duty in Norfolk, Virginia, where I spent eight hours a day (or night) in charge of a communications section consisting of five or six White men and two or three African Americans. The services had been integrated for a long time, so I wasn't expecting any trouble. One night, one of the Black men asked a White man for a drag on his cigarette. The White man handed it over with the good-natured injunction "Don't n—lip it." I braced to break up a fight, but the Black man merely chuckled and said, "I won't."

One evening, Dr. King was expected to speak at a rally for civil rights. My wife and I went and found that we were almost the only Whites in a crowd of several hundred people. The master of ceremonies had to announce that Dr. King would not be able to come. A lot of people got up to leave, but the MC cried, "If you leave now, you are a traitor to the cause." We stayed put. They started to pass the plate. "We're gettin' respectable," cried the MC. "We don't want no noisy money in the plate! We want dignified money." I put ten dollars in, which was generous (I thought) at the time.

At one point during my service, one of the Black men in my watch section was promoted to first-class petty officer. A White second-class petty officer, growing old in the service, came to me and said, "Mr. Vinson, I don't think that I can take orders from a Black man." The proper response would have been to tell him to take it to the commander of the personnel unit, a gruff old lieutenant commander who had come up through the hawsepipe.[10] It was not my problem. But instead, I had one of those inspired moments when you do or say just the right thing to the right person at the right time. It was as if someone much wiser were speaking through me. I asked, "How many men are in this section?"

10. That is, who had begun his career as an enlisted man.

"Nine," he replied.

"How many coffee cups do we have?"

"Six."

"Okay, you know you've drunk out of the same coffee cup he has. Are you really going to tell me that you can't take orders from him?"

There was no answer and no problem.

In the previous chapter, I told a story about my sister riding on a segregated bus in Little Rock in the 1940s. I'm going to close this chapter with a friend's story of his first ride on an integrated bus.

Ed Brewer, an artist, boarded a city bus on the first day of the service's integration. He sat down on one of the bench seats in front, leaving a space between him and another White man. At the next stop, a little Black schoolboy got on, dropped his fare in the box, and surveyed the seats. It was clear that his Momma had scrubbed and ironed him within an inch of his life, and equally clear that she had told him that he could sit anywhere he wanted on that bus from now on, and no White man could make him move to the back.

The little boy walked straight to the seat between Ed and the other man and clambered up onto it. Then he looked at Ed, and Ed looked at him (and probably smiled, because Ed was that kind of guy). Then, the little boy looked at the other White man, and the White man looked at him. And then, the little boy, as if overcome by his own boldness, just bowed his head. All the grown-ups chuckled and the bus went happily on its way.

Chapter 4

Take Me to the Border[1]

A FTER the navy, I entered graduate school and then embarked on a long career of teaching classics and archaeology. Through a series of bad decisions and progressive alcoholism, I landed at the University of Arizona in Tucson, where I deservedly failed to get tenure. I sobered up in 1979, and by 1986 had recovered enough to get involved in the Sanctuary Movement. It was here that I encountered, firsthand and for the first time, what racism and oppression meant as a daily life-and-death matter to those who suffered from them. As part of this, I began to learn the real meaning of America's gunboat diplomacy in Latin America, our systematic repression of democracy there, and what Porfirio Diaz, former president of Mexico, meant when he said, "Poor Mexico! So far from God and so close to the United States!"[2]

The influx of migrants and refugees coming to the United States in recent years has alarmed those who are unfamiliar with the border or with Latin America and US policy there. Former President Trump, Senator Ted Cruz, and their epigones have exploited Americans' fear and unfamiliarity for political gain. The fact is, though, that American ranchers and farmers on the border

1. The title of a song by Tucson musician and impresario Ted Warmbrand, used by permission.
2. Carroll, "So Far from God," para. 6.

have profited from the cheap labor of Latin Americans for genera-tions, and American consumers have, too, at the supermarket.

As an observer of the border for the last forty-eight years, I believe that the American "farm" (read "plantation") owner grow-ing cash crops for profit wants to continue the situation as it is. He has a large workforce of insecure hands to whom he can offer minimal wages, substandard living and working conditions, and minimal to nonexistent sanitation. This ensures his maximum profit. Any migrant worker who asks for better wages or condi-tions can be pointed out to the authorities and swiftly deported.

On the other hand, work permits, a living wage, enough porta potties, washing stations, and decent quarters for the work-men would either blow a big hole in the plantation owner's profit or would mean a big jump in consumer prices.

It is true that migrants leave a lot of trash and scare Ameri-can border dwellers. When the smugglers pick up the migrants on the US side, they force the latter to discard absolutely every-thing so that they (the smugglers) can cram as many as possible into their vans to drive to safe houses from which the migrants are distributed to the plantations. These overcrowded vans often get into high-speed chases with the Border Patrol or state police, resulting in crashes fatal to many migrants. We have found piles of backpacks, clothes, identification papers, baby carriages, food, and electrolyte bottles at the pick-up points. And frightened, hungry, lost people often scare lonely ranchers as they loom up out of the dusk on the border.

Migrants cross as they do because big American money wants it that way. It's cheaper than paying a few extra dollars in taxes for a humane, safe system. As for the drug dealers, most cross through established, guarded ports of entry, and anyway, who buys the drugs? And how is it that this huge volume of drugs gets through closely guarded ports of entry?

When my grandfather was a young man, he worked as an accountant and ran a company store on a big cotton plantation in Arkansas (see page 25). I learned early on how the system works, and it makes no difference whether the workers are African

Americans, Latin Americans, or (for that matter) German POWs, of whom we had a plethora during World War II.

Refugees are a different matter. Despite Donald Trump's fulminations to the contrary, the Sanctuary Movement in the 1980s arose spontaneously among American citizens struggling to save the lives of Latin American (mostly Central American) refugees. They fled (and flee today) their homelands in fear for their lives.

This comes about because the US supports murderous dictatorships that torture and kill people for objecting to political repression and extortion. These dictatorships are heavily in debt to organizations like the World Bank and the International Monetary Fund. These financial ogres lend money to small, poor countries to grow cash crops like coffee or sugar cane, rather than food crops which might feed their people. The US also has a trade deal with Canada and Mexico which allows the northern countries to dump their subsidized crops of (for example) corn and potatoes in Mexico to drive unsubsidized Mexican crops off the market. Farmers in Latin America naturally resent all of this, so the US and the financial ogres find dictatorships preferable to democracy in order to maintain "stability." Besides, dictatorships buy huge quantities of weapons and munitions from us.

Therefore, we train Latin American police and military in torture and repression at Fort Benning in Georgia, at the Western Hemisphere Institute of Security (WHINSEC, formerly the School of the Americas). Any hungry Latin American brave or foolish enough to protest this system is labeled a Communist, and therefore he and his family are subject to arrest, torture, and death.[3]

The system today is made much worse by gangs which have their origin in the United States, an unpleasant fact which I shall explain later.[4]

To return to the Sanctuary Movement in the '80s and '90s: the Border Patrol often caught and deported refugees to their

---

3. Archbishop Hélder Câmara wrote, "When I give food to the poor, they call me a saint. When I ask why the poor have no food, they call me a communist" ("Dom Helder Camara").

4. See pp. 52, 53 of this book.

countries of origin, where many were tortured and/or killed. Occasionally, large groups of ten or twenty got lost in the ferocious Sonoran Desert that spreads across northern Mexico and the southwestern United States. There, in summer, the temperature of the desert floor reaches 140 degrees. Even if you can find water (for the most part, there is none), it is physically impossible to carry as much as you need. Of such groups, perhaps half die; the US Border Patrol deports whatever survivors they find.[5] In the '80s and '90s, perhaps as many as 5–10 percent of those returned to Central America or Pinochet's Chile would be killed by the authorities for having belonged to a labor union, for having somehow expressed discontent with the regime, or simply for having been returned home without papers. Today, the gangs (with their protection rackets, drugs, and prostitution) are waiting for them.

Eventually, deaths, newspaper articles, and news stories on television reached such a pitch that a Quaker goatherd named Jim Corbett and a Presbyterian minister named John Fife got involved and organized a rescue mission. Jim (who had an MA in philosophy from Harvard) was the theoretician of the group, and his rationale went like this: US law declared that foreigners fleeing their own countries because of a well-founded fear of persecution had a right to claim political asylum here and to have a hearing before a judge. At the time, the US was denying this remedy to refugees from Haiti and Latin America while allowing it to refugees from Eastern Europe, especially from Communist countries. This was clearly discrimination on racial and political grounds (the US assumed that refugees from Latin America were Communists), discrimination which, if challenged in the courts, could be shown to be illegal—i.e., the US was violating its own law. Helping the refugees to exercise their right to claim asylum in the

---

5. President Biden's policy is similar to Trump's, continuing the "remain in Mexico" policy and complicated by the desire to exclude foreigners who might have COVID-19 and by huge groups of migrants, like the thirteen thousand Haitians now (September 18, 2021) at Del Rio, Texas. Biden has drunk the Republican Kool-Aid, using mounted, cursing Border Patrol to ride down defenseless Haitians and deporting masses of them back to Haiti, reminiscent of federal practice under G. H. W. Bush in 1992.

US—their right to a lawyer and a hearing before a judge—was not, therefore, illegal; it was not civil disobedience. Rather, it was civil obedience—Jim, John, and their advisors and coreligionists would actually be ensuring that the US enforced its own law fairly.

The group that Jim and John organized quickly developed into a large network. Carlos in El Salvador, for example, might have had a family member killed and threats made against him for labor-union activities, for something he had published, or for attending a demonstration. He would flee. If he were lucky, he might hear en route about an office in Mexico City where a lady would ask him some questions and then refer him to a church in northern Mexico—in Chihuahua City, for example, or Hermosillo. Once he got there, the pastor would call Southside Presbyterian Church in Tucson. There, a couple of elderly ladies, Amy Schubitz and Marianna Neill, fielded twelve thousand urgent requests for help over the years for rescue teams, doctors, lawyers, diapers, and formula, and let John Fife use his office when they weren't busy. They sent someone down to Nogales or Hermosillo or Chihuahua to ask Carlos some more questions, and then, in due course, a couple of volunteers drove down into Mexico to bring Carlos up to the border. The crossing point was usually miles out in the desert, but a walk of only a few kilometers to the fence.

Since it was illegal to actually help Carlos across the border (in those innocent days, a wobbly cattle fence consisting of three strands of barbed wire), another group would meet him on the US side and take him on a short walk to their car. Then, they would drive him to a safe house in Tucson, a perfectly legal proceeding, since it was permitted to take him to a prearranged appointment with his attorney. The whole trip from, say, San Salvador to Tucson, Arizona, might take as much as four months for a poor man who had to work his way.

In 1986, I read in the newspaper about the arrests of the Sanctuary Eleven, consisting of Rev. John Fife, several other clergymen, Jim Corbett, and several other laypeople. I had done nothing significant during the civil rights movement or during the Vietnam era—from timidity and because it would have interfered with my drinking—but now, sober, confronted with so many deaths result-ing from my nation's racial injustice, and a rescue mission right under my nose, I knew I had to do something, and here was a church that walked its talk. I went to Southside to volunteer and was met with considerable suspicion. I learned later that the US government had recently recruited a spy to attend church services and infiltrate planning meetings of the Tucson Refugee Support Group (TRSG), which organized trips to the border and cared for the refugees. Nevertheless, I found my way to the TRSG's of-fice, where I was put to stuffing envelopes. I started showing up at Southside's Sunday services and at demonstrations in front of the Federal Building in downtown Tucson. After a few months of this apprenticeship, I was actually called to take a refugee from the Mexican church where he was sheltering to the border fence, out in the country. My Spanish was minimal. I had had a few lessons, and I am fluent in Italian, so I could read the newspaper and buy lunch, but real conversation, like "Why are you traveling with this Salvadoran?" was still difficult for me.

On this particular trip, two other Anglos and I drove from Tucson to the Mexican church in a ratty old pickup. We collected the Salvadoran refugee, and then I drove the three of them to a drop-off point near the fence, where the crew on the American side would pick him up and take him to, in this case, Southside Presbyterian Church. There, he would have a cramped but dry and secure place to stay until he met with his lawyer. I dropped them off, and then had an hour or so to kill until picking up the two Anglos again to return to the US.

I drove around, looking at the scenery and taking a few pic-tures, and blundered right into a Mexican army roadblock. They wanted to know what I was doing there. I was driving someone else's truck, was carrying a Salvadoran passport (I had stuffed it under the mess on the cab's floor), and had no Salvadoran to go with it. My Spanish evaporated into "turista" and "fotografía." The soldiers were correct, clean, and polished, but as they searched the truck, looking for drugs, they were grinning. It wasn't everyday they got to collar a Yankee, and I was sure that I was going to a

Mexican jail. The worst was the knowledge that I had let my friends down and gotten an expensive piece of property impounded.

But the soldiers let me go! They didn't find the passport or any contraband in the jackets my friends had left in the truck, nor did they ask for the truck's registration, so they let me go. But they wouldn't let me go back toward the pickup point. I would have to wait. So, I drove down the road a mile or so and parked, waiting until they went home for lunch. When they did, I drove back up the mountain and apologized profusely to my friends for being so late. They were very understanding.

That was the first of many such trips I made over the next four or five years. I made other mistakes, but none as bad as that first one. Like the time I got the truck stuck in the Santa Cruz River. At least we could wade ashore and ask a pickup full of passing ranchers for help. I did some things right, too. Like the time I was carrying a Guatemalan mother and her three small children as we approached a known roadblock deep in Mexico. I gave her an American newspaper to unfold and pretend to read and made sure that she held it right side up. An American grandmother straight off a Norman Rockwell cover was in the passenger seat beside me. To cap it all, a commercial bus appeared in my rearview mirror. I slowed down and waved it past. When we got to the roadblock, the Mexican customs officials were all busy with the bus riders and waved us through without question.

In 1991, I started teaching at Pima Community College in Tucson, Arizona. I taught humanities ("dead White men," my daughter calls it) and art history. After a while, ironically, I was assigned a course called Multicultural Perspectives, a course in the experience of people of color in the United States. At first, I was nervous: I was a well-paid White male. What right did I have to teach people of color about their families' own experiences in this country? But, I had grown up with the oppression of Blacks. And I had lived in Tucson long enough to know something of the local prejudice against Hispanics and Native Americans: the city had destroyed several Hispanic neighborhoods in order to build a convention center, then spent thirty-five years (I'm not exaggerating) wondering how to revitalize downtown. My church, Southside Presbyterian, had been founded by Tohono O'Odham, Native Americans who had been kicked out of a White Presbyterian church and therefore started their own. When they called a Black pastor many years later, he insisted that the church integrate— i.e., include Whites. From Mae and Henry Tanabe, who cared for me during my childhood, I knew about the oppression of Asian Americans.

In the end, the students taught me. Some Native Americans and Hispanics had gone to White boarding schools, and their teachers had beaten them for speaking Apache, or Navajo, or Spanish, because as little children, they knew no other language. One was from Bhutan and told us of the prejudice he had encountered in Pakistan. During summer vacations, my wife guided me on trips around the American West. We went to the Little Bighorn Battlefield National Monument twice, returning the second time to see the beautiful new Native American memorial. We went to Wounded Knee, site of the last massacre of the American Indian Wars, where the Seventh Cavalry got its revenge for the Little Bighorn by slaughtering about three hundred Native American men (few armed and that poorly), women, and children. Their cemetery now occupies the little rise where the American commander placed his battery of artillery. We went to the grave of Sacajawea, who contributed so much to the Lewis and Clark expedition by securing them horses at the most critical moment. My wife has visited Aravaipa Canyon, where White Tucsonans, armed with weapons furnished by local hero Sam Hughes, massacred a party of peaceful Native Americans under the United States flag.

In 1987, Linda Ronstadt released *Canciones De Mi Padre*, her groundbreaking phonograph record of Mexican folk songs. The Ronstadts are an old Mexican Tucson family—Tucson was Mexican until the Gadsden Purchase in 1853—and they were a power in the town. Pete was chief of police, Mike ran the hardware store, and Linda was breaking records. I bought a cassette tape (remember those?) of the record and played it in the car for the refugees. One song, "El Corrido de Cananea," was a big hit, known all over

Latin America from Mexico to Chile (Pete and Mike sing backup). It tells of a self-styled tough guy who gets arrested in Agua Prieta, just across the border from Douglas, Arizona. The police take him to jail in Cananea, a small copper-mining town way up in the mountains. One verse in particular always got a laugh: "The sheriffs arrested me / In the American style. / Like a real criminal / All armed to the teeth."[6] Sometimes, I had to drive refugees from Agua Prieta to Nogales and took precisely that road. The refugees used to sing along with Linda as we drove through the saguaro cactus and then up through the manzanita and alligator juniper to the vast piles of slag around Cananea, then back down to the saguaros again around Imuris and Nogales. One time, my passengers were a Salvadoran and his daughter who had made hand grenades for the Salvadoran rebels. We sang "El Corrido de Cananea," and when that ended, the father started singing English Christmas carols, so we sang those for a while. Another time, I was carrying a mother and two little children. I gave the children stuffed animals, and many years later at a Christmas party, someone told me that the little girl, by then a ravishing beauty of eighteen or nineteen, still had her stuffed bear.

Romance bloomed, sometimes successfully. Two Anglo friends of mine married refugees and have raised lovely families. One child is our goddaughter. Her father was a union man and had to flee. One child (a cousin, if I remember rightly) was beaten so severely by the Salvadoran National Guard that he remains developmentally disabled. For a while, after the civil war ended, the family was able to visit relatives in El Salvador, but now it is too dangerous again because of the gangs.

You may have heard of the gangs of El Salvador, Guatemala, and Honduras. In the '80s and '90s, there were savage civil wars in El Salvador and Guatemala. Hungry farmers and shopkeepers with bolt-action rifles tried to protect themselves against the modern armies and SWAT teams of dictators armed with the latest

---

6. My translation. Original: "Me aprehendieron los gendarmes / Al estilo americano, / Como un hombre de delito, / Todos con pistola en mano" (Ronstadt, "Corrido de Cananea," para. 3).

American technology. The authorities' attitude was exemplified by a photograph I saw of a dead "insurgent" dumped under a sign advertising insecticide.

Honduras was known as "the land of perpetual maneuvers," because American armed forces trained there for potential action in the other countries, for what is called "counterinsurgency war-fare" or "low-intensity warfare.[7] Part of the training, also carried out at WHINSEC at Fort Benning in Georgia, consisted of water-boarding (near drowning of the prisoner) or electric shocks to the most sensitive parts of the body, and teaching these valuable skills to Latin American police and military. Families flee this sort of treatment. Some make their way to the United States, where they may or may not be granted political asylum (almost certainly not under Trump, doubtfully under Obama, more likely under Biden). If not, they may stay illegally in the US, eking out a precarious exis-tence in the shadows. Their children may be captured and deport-ed by the US authorities. Back in Central America, the deportees inevitably turn to extortion, pimping, and the protection racket, all enforced with extreme brutality.[8] The US will never acknowledge its responsibility for this problem, and so will never take any ac-tion or pay a dime to solve it. This is the background against which my remarkable goddaughter trains to be a pediatrician.

The Sanctuary Movement was my field research and my li-brary. I brought all these lessons to class and became a much more truthful teacher as a result.

The movement continued until 1990, when a lawsuit, Ameri-can Baptist Churches v. Thornburgh, went against the government. In its decision, the court allowed half a million (yes, you read that correctly) refugees not merely to remain in the United States but to work as well until their individual cases could be settled. Jim Corbett had been right all along (philosophers are dangerous). The

7. In fact, the situation on the border since the 1980s has met the US Army's definition of "low-intensity warfare" (Wikipedia, s.v. "Low-intensity conflict," https://en.wikipedia.org/wiki/Low-intensity_conflict).

8. See Nolan, "I've Lost Everything" (a review article on books about the gangs).

United States had violated its own policy of political asylum. Now it was hoist by its own petard. Congress will never appropriate enough money to hire enough lawyers and judges to process half a million asylum cases—and that was thirty years ago. How many more asylum cases have backed up under Trump's blatantly racist policies!

I also spent eighteen months photographing the appalling conditions in which Latin American workers have to live as they labor in US factories' "twin plants" in Nogales, Mexico.[9]

In 2000, because migrants continued to die in the desert, Tucson's clergy and interested layfolk met at a Quaker meeting house. The result was that they encouraged a newcomer, Rev. Robin Hoover, to take action. He set up Humane Borders. This is a very different organization. Its chief aim is to rescue the migrant wandering in the desert, whatever his status or nationality, especially during the deadly summers. In its simplest form, the group sets out fifty-five-gallon drums of water at points in the desert where migrants are known to have died, with blue flags on thirty-foot poles to mark the barrels' locations. These are filled by a fleet of tanker trucks that roar and grind their way over the unpaved (and very rocky) roads to the barrels every three or four days. The tankers are loaded with first-aid gear, blankets, and packets of snacks. More than once, we have gone home from these missions without hats, shirts, or socks, sometimes without shoes and often without money, knowing that we can easily get more but that the migrant was near death. On one occasion, we searched for and found the body of an eighteen-year-old Guatemalan girl, Prudencia Martín Gomez, who had become ill and was abandoned by her smugglers. Someone noted and called the number on the telephone pole under which she lay down to die.

I have crouched in the dust to wash and bandage blistered feet, and my years of teaching and articles about archaeology are as smoke by comparison.

9. See Vinson, "Los Tapiros."

Chapter 5

Digging Up Roots

A ROUND 1990, my interest in my family's history revived because of the death of my father in 1989 and because my mother was sending me piles of family photographs. Long before, she had sent me painted portraits on cardboard of my paternal great-grandfather, Lt. Exum Vinson, and his wife, Molly, he in his Confederate uniform and she in a red dress with two broad blue stripes that (when she sat) was suggestive of the Confederate battle flag. But now I had the photographs from which the paintings had been copied, ambrotypes (glass plates) tinted with pink patches on the cheeks and gold for the buttons and braid. Mother also sent the family Bible, fourteen pounds of board (and I mean planks) bound with leather, embossed in gilt with Noah's ark and the ark of the covenant on the front, and containing parallel texts of both the King James Version and the Revised Standard Version on pages measuring nine by twelve inches. In it, in clear copperplate script, either Exum or Molly, or maybe a great-aunt, had written the names and dates of their parents' history: Jesse Vinson (Exum's father) had married Elizabeth Futrell, and Molly's parents were a J. D. L. Vaughan[1] and Sarah Edwards.

---

1. Jonathan deLoach Vaughan. De Loach is a Huguenot name, and this impressed Aunt Ruth, who seems to have traced the family through its female line. She was a feminist avant la lettre.

I had some trouble with the old records. My grandmother Vinson had given me Exum's Confederate service record (along with that of her father, a Williams), which she had gotten from the National Archives, and it listed his place of enlistment as Wheelersville, in Northampton County, North Carolina. A quick look at the atlas showed that there is no Wheelersville in Northampton County. Someone in the North Carolina archives suggested Wheeler's Mill, now Barrow's Mill Pond, near Jackson, near the Virginia line, in the northeast of the state. Perhaps the recruiting officer had misheard the name, or perhaps the Yankees who captured Exum got it wrong. I ended up having a lengthy and productive correspondence with a Mrs. Roye, who worked in Jackson's little library. Jesse (Exum's father), I discovered, lived on Bear Swamp, southeast of Jackson, and was illiterate, signing his marriage bond with an X. He died intestate, leaving 144 acres (almost a whole section of land), which the state duly divided among his three children and a man named Levi Flythe (two of Exum's sisters married two Flythe brothers, who had served in Exum's company during the war). For a long time, I was stuck there, unable to get back any further.

One damp Christmas season, my oldest daughter and I went to North Carolina, Virginia, Maryland, and Pennsylvania to look at the records and tour the battlefields. We didn't get far with the records (apart from settling the origin of the name Exum), but we did tour Sharpsburg (Antietam), Fredericksburg, and Gettysburg, where our great- and twice great-grandfathers had fought. On another trip, too, we went to Silver Spring, Maryland, where Papa had his accident and was injured in the limb, as Aunt Blanche delicately put it.[2] Exum's regiment (the Thirty-Second North Carolina Infantry) was on garrison duty for the first two years of the war—this was when he taught himself to read and write and earned his commission. The 1860 census lists Exum as illiterate, so his learning to read and write was a real triumph.

---

2. "Limb" was a Victorian euphemism for "leg." Humans and pianos had limbs. Livestock had legs.

Grandmother Vinson's father fought at Sharpsburg,[3] Fredericksburg, and Gettysburg. He was First Sergeant James Vincent Williams, Company K, Third Arkansas, Hood's Texas Brigade. His daughter, my grandmother Vinson, claimed that he was descended from Roger Williams, founder of Rhode Island, but I have not been able to check this yet. Ironically, after looking over the battlefield at Fredericksburg, my daughter and I took in a movie about Malcolm X that evening.

When I checked up on the Williamses, Grandmother Vinson's family, I found that they were quite wealthy and had owned a lot of slaves. My father had not known. Possibly, Grandmother had not either, though she always referred contemptuously to the "Great Emancipator" as "that old Lincoln." In the inconsistent system of Confederate record keeping, Arkansas's military records contain the recruit's place of birth, whereas North Carolina's do not, and Sgt. Williams was born in Robertson County, Tennessee, north of Nashville, almost on the Kentucky line. I took this information to Springfield, the county seat, and soon I was up to my knees in family records. The Williamses had been quite wealthy. Sgt. Williams's father left him one slave and five hundred dollars. When Sgt. Williams reached his majority, he up and left for Arkansas. What he did with the slave is not recorded. He might have taken the slave with him, or he might have sold him (or her) to raise cash for settling in his adopted state. This must have been during the census of 1860, as neither the census takers in Tennessee nor those in Arkansas caught up with him before he settled near Monticello, Arkansas. A year later, when the war broke out, he enlisted at Hamburg, not far from Monticello, which is why, 130-plus years later, I was driving to the Third Arkansas's museum in Hamburg[4] when I passed the monument erected by the Nisei.

---

3. Known as Antietam to Northerners after the creek that runs through the battlefield. Confederates named their battles after the nearest courthouse (e.g., Manassas, Sharpsburg); Yankees named theirs after the nearest watercourse (Bull Run, Antietam). Gettysburg is used by both sides; it would be hard to pay proper reverence to Plum Run.

4. The Third Arkansas was the name eventually given to the regiment raised in Hamburg, Arizona, where its museum is located.

For a long time, I let matters rest there. I had corrected two mistakes in the family history: there had once been money on the Williams's side of the family, and they had once owned slaves. I also knew that when Exum moved to Arkansas, he had joined the Klan. This piece of information came from a second cousin, Catherine Washburn, in Tucson, Arizona, where she lived with her mother, Aunt Fanny (Frances Vinson Dungan, née Gordon). Aunt Fanny remembered stories from Reconstruction, told to her by her aunt Laura Shell. Aunt Fanny was in her late nineties and early hundreds (she died at 104, less a few days) when I knew her and her daughter, and was too frail to tell all of the stories, so over a couple of days, Cousin Katherine agreed to tell them to my tape recorder, and the following is what she told me. "Tell me about Cora," I say. There is a large oil portrait of a little girl hanging on the wall behind Aunt Fanny.

Great-Aunt Fanny in front of little Cora's portrait

"Well, that's not a Vinson yarn, that's a Snow thing." To be honest, I don't know how the Snows and Shells were related.

"Cousin Cora lived in Tennessee . . . beautiful country now. The rest of the family had gone down to Arkansas.[5] During the Civil War, Cora's mother lived there on this farm, and she was alone, of course—all the men were in the war. And this Yankee officer came thoo (an' he 'uz drunk), and he knocked Cora across the room and was goin' to rape her mother when this ole Nigra who worked for 'em ('uz a slave of course at that time) killed him." Katherine's accent becomes deeply Southern as she gets into these stories, as if she is remembering "Aint"[6] Laura's voice from so long ago. When the officer threw Cora across the room, she suffered internal injuries that eventually killed her.

"How did he kill him?"

"Well, the story doesn't say how he killed him. Anyway, he killed him. But he knew and they knew that killin' a Yankee officer, they better all get outta there. So, he hid Cora and her mother under some corn shucks in the back of the wagon, an' bein' Black, he could get thoo the Yankee lines. He was an escapin' slave goin' to freedom. An' they traveled that way an' hid out where they could, an' ate what they could off the land, an' got up to New York to Southern sympathizers, an' see, he could get 'em there all right. Well, that's when the portrait was painted in New York. Cora was about two years old when the portrait was made, an' she died a short time later."

In White men's fiction about the war, Yankees don't act like the officer who murdered Cora. The gallant Yankee officer who chases Bayard Sartoris and Ringo in Faulkner's *The Unvanquished* is gallant John Sartoris in a blue uniform, right down to the irony. Even the sugan[7] Bailey in Benét's *John Brown's Body* redeems him-

---

5. The move to Arkansas occurred "in the year the stars fell," according to a typewritten, unsigned note that some forgotten family member put with a piece of silk that one of the Shells or Snows had woven. An unusually heavy Perseid meteor shower happened in the early 1860s, so I suppose it's just possible that the family somehow managed to move from Tennessee to Arkansas before Grant captured Memphis and Vicksburg. Of course, it's also possible that they moved long before the war.

6. I have written it "Aint" to capture Cousin Katherine's accent.

7. "Sugan" was Scots dialect for a coarse rope made of twisted heather; it

self by not stealing the Southern aristocrat's fancy scissors. Clearly, American men cannot stomach the fact that we rape, murder children, and steal in wartime. But women know the truth.

Cousin Katherine's second story is, in many ways, a mirror of the first, as if Cora and her mother had incurred a debt that their slave's mere freedom did not cancel, a debt that God (or whoever handles these things) decided would be paid by the Arkansas branch of the family—that is, by the family of Katherine's great-aunt Laura Shell.

Katherine starts by telling how Laura's father came home from the war. "Well, they came stragglin' in; they had to walk or hitch a wagon ride, or whatever they could do. So, many of the men had already come in. Well, there was evidently a long lane from their house down to the front gate to where the wagons could come. An' so little Laura would go down to the gate every afternoon just before sunset and stand there an' wait for Papa to come home until dark. An' the others would tell her, 'Well . . . Papa's not comin' back, Laura. Everybody's come back, but Papa's not comin' back.' Laura wouldn't believe it. An' she'd go back to the gate (an' she 'uz probably five years old then), an' she'd go back home, and then she'd be back next day watchin' for Papa. An' then one day, here came Papa. An' Laura was the first to greet him."

In 1865, Arkansas was ravaged not just by Union armies (which included five thousand Black troops from Arkansas[8]) but by jayhawkers and bushwhackers, the deserters and guerrillas of both sides. The Ku Klux Klan had not yet been organized. Men were just ex-Confederate soldiers, barely home from the war, presumably bitter and angry, and frightened at the changes: slaves freed, the Yankees in occupation, civil authority in disarray.

"There was no Ku Klux Klan," Katherine continues. "The Blacks had all been freed, so they said. An' here came the carpetbaggers.

---

became a word for a trashy, coarse person (*Webster's Third International Dictionary* [1967], s.v. "sugan"). E.g., "They may wear nice clothes and ride on the train, but they're sugans, just the same."

8. Ashmore, *Arkansas*, 79. See chapters 9 and 10 for the details of a rowdy and corrupt Reconstruction and its aftermath.

An' there was so much disturbance. An' Aint Laura's father went down to the kitchen one morning to start the fire in the wood stove, an' he felt or heard something back of him, an' he turned, and this Nigra man was standing there with a big stick of stove-wood. Well, Pa shot him but din' kill him, and the Black man ran. So then, Pa and the other White men got together. Well, they knew in their area Blacks had not shown any signs of disturbances, but they knew that they would; there was goin' to be trouble; the carpetbaggers was comin' through. So, they formed the first Ku Klux Klan in that area. An' that, as Aint Laura told it to me, was more to scare 'em. I said, 'Aint Laura, din' they have any lynchins?' She said, 'Hon, they got thu scarin' 'em, they wasn't anybody to lynch! They either left or behaved themselves.' So far as I know, there were never any lynchings in that area."

Which can't be true. For a century after the Civil War, the story of race relations in the US was built on the twin lies that the slaves were free and that it was always someone else who did the lynching. The rest of the story is not on tape, so I tell it as nearly as possible the way Katherine told it to me.

"Carpetbaggers" was originally a term for unscrupulous adventurers from the North who moved South after the Civil War to exploit the economic and social chaos of what Naomi Klein has called "disaster capitalism."[9] Here, Cousin Katherine (or "Aint" Laura) blames them for fomenting social unrest among the newly freed African Americans. For example, a New Yorker named Daniel P. Upham arrived in Arkansas in 1865 with ten dollars in his pocket, but with valuable connections to the Union general commanding the area around the river port of DeValls Bluff. Using his influence, Upham managed to lease two thousand acres of cotton land and hire the men and mules to work them. Within a year, his profit was estimated between $200,000 and $300,000.[10] The Klan was formed in 1866, perhaps by the former Confederate cavalry leader and slave dealer Nathan Bedford Forrest. It was, really, a continuation of the Civil War by guerrilla, having as its purpose

9. Klein, "How Power Profits," para. 23.
10. *Ashmore, Arkansas*, 95.

the oppression of African Americans and using the most violent means to do so, including pitched battles with Union forces (often Black troops).

Laura's papa told how he and the other men robed themselves and their horses and muffled their horses' hooves. Then, just at dusk, they rode up to the cabin of some Black man whom they considered a troublemaker—i.e. who wanted to vote or, worse, run for office. The Blacks wouldn't hear the Klansmen coming; they'd just hear the dogs barking and look out the window, and the yard would be full of ghostly figures. Then, the Klansmen called the man out, and the leader would say, "Boy, I just come from hell, and I'm thirsty. Get me a bucket of water." When the man handed him the bucket, the leader poured the water into a funnel connected to a large bladder hidden under his horse's robe. Thus, he appeared to be drinking the whole bucket of water. He'd hand it back and say, "I'm still thirsty; get me another." When the man complied, the Klansman would appear to drink that one, but usually before he had finished, the Black man had fled. This must have been a common trick; D. W. Griffith portrays it in *Birth of a Nation*.[11] Sometimes, the Klansman would have an artificial arm up his sleeve. He would offer to shake hands with the "free and equal" Black, and the arm would come away in the victim's grasp.

The Klansmen may or may not have believed that the robes and juvenile tricks scared the Blacks (who were popularly thought to fear ghosts and "hants," but of course the victims knew exactly who the Klansmen were and knew they'd be burnt out, tortured, and killed by familiar Whites, not by ghosts, whether they believed in the latter or not.

Sometime after Laura's papa joined the Klan, he stood with his little daughter by the gate of his front yard one evening under a big oak tree. In the last of the daylight, he was as innocent of God's grace as he was of God's ironic humor, both of which were about to befall him. He and Laura watched a group of agents of the Freedmen's Bureau trot past, escorted by Yankee cavalry. Then,

11. Griffith, *Birth of a Nation*.

a panicky crowd of freedmen came running after the horsemen, "screamin' and hollerin'," said Katherine, quoting "Aint" Laura.

It was the same problem that plagued every Union soldier in the South; freeing slaves was one thing, but feeding and caring for four million freedmen was something else again. The army was not organized to do that, hadn't counted on that, and badly wanted the freedmen to go somewhere else—the White House, perhaps, or back to the plantations where, in the end, most of them did go.[12] So, when the nominally freed and hungry slaves saw agents of the Freedmen's Bureau riding with the Union army, of course they ran after. Here was the possibility of real freedom, the promise of forty acres and a mule—at the very least, a day's rations.

And then, Papa and the little girl saw this: a Black mother, hungry, ragged, her toddler running beside her, too small to keep up and too big to tote. The mother yelled to the baby, "Come on, come on!" But the baby cried and couldn't run fast enough. Suddenly, the mother picked the baby up, swung him by the feet, and smashed his head against the tree trunk. There was a crunch, a splash of red, then the mother dropped the dead baby and ran on.

A second Black mother with a toddler shrieked at Laura's father, "I cain't do what she done. You take him!" She thrust her child into the arms of the dumfounded Confederate veteran and ran after the Freedmen's Bureau. Laura's papa was left holding one Black baby while the other lay dead.

It occurs to me that those two babies must have been the children of rape by the mothers' White masters, or soldiers, or any man who happened along in the chaos of war and collapse. That would go a long way to explain the inexplicable and the justice of the Black mother's giving the baby to a White man. The Shells reckoned the baby was about three. "Very simple people," says Isak Dinesen, "seem to have a talent for adopting children, and feeling towards them as if they were their own."[13] The family kept the boy.

---

12. One Union general at Helena solved his problem by swapping Blacks to planters for cotton, two per bale, which could be sold at a handsome profit (Ashmore, *Arkansas*, 95).

13. Dinesen, *Out of Africa*, 11.

"Why?" I ask. "There must have been lots of Black families who . . ."

"She gave him to them," says Katherine, as if that settles the matter, as if the gift conferred an obligation that went far beyond the boundaries of Black and White. She goes on with her story. About this time, the Union army decided to put down the Klan. As Katherine tells it, "The carpetbaggers knew that the Klan was being formed, so they were rounding up the White men in the area and confining them in a kind of prison thing, so they were going from house to house, calling out the White male of that family."

"And this was with the help of the Union army?" One hundred and thirty years after the event, Katherine considers carpetbaggers and Yankee soldiers to be the same thing.

"Yeah. They called for Laura's papa. Papa wasn't home, but Uncle Melvin was, and he was the White male head of the house. So, they took him out in the field and shot him. Instead of makin' him a prisoner, they just shot him. He wouldn't tell where Papa was. So, Aint Laura and her cousin climbed up on the pigsty, an' the pigsty roof slanted, an' they lay there lookin' out so they could see the flash of the guns and tell them where Uncle Melvin's body was, so the pigs wouldn't get it.

"Papa came home from the Klan meetin'. They all packed up and went to the hills. Well, they took the little Nigra boy with 'em. They couldn't leave him! They took Uncle Melvin's body and hid it under corn shucks an' went on up into the hills. They din' dare stop to try to bury him while they were goin' up. They made it, traveling by moonlight an' very early in the morning, and then they hid out in the woods.

"They stayed there long enough to form a school, because there were other Whites that came up in there. Up in that part, there was no slave question; those hill people din' have slaves. This little Nigra boy stayed there long enough that he grew and went to school with the other children, and then he later became a very well known circuit-rider preacher."

Of course he did. What other profession could he follow? Isaac thrust upon an unready Abraham—only God could explain his life to him.

Katherine stops. Question as I might then or later, she remembers nothing else. Later, she explains that the killing of Uncle Melvin and the gift of the baby took place on the same day, that the family kept the child because they had to flee and there was no time to look for a Black family for him, and there were none up in the hills. "Well," I said, unable to take in what I imagined to be the contradiction of an ex-Confederate, a Klansman, adopting a Black baby, "they could have found a family for him if they wanted to."

"Well, I guess they din' want to," said Katherine, "because they kept him for quite a few years. I don't know just how long."

I often think about Cora and the Black baby. Their stories contain a riddle that I cannot read. Obviously, the slave who rescued Cora and her mother fled North for his freedom, but he didn't have to take the White folks any more than the Shells had to take the Black toddler. Since the Shells sent the child to school (with White children, yet!), they treated him better than a slave. Perhaps they loved him, but we don't know how he felt about them. The stories are incomplete, because they lack the Blacks' point of view. They also both serve the White myth that Master was always kind and that good slaves loved Master in return. But in truth, Master was not kind by definition, and Papa Shell had just risked death for four years to keep slaves in their place. Perhaps the sudden murder and gift marked a spiritual conversion for him.

It is very telling that neither Katherine nor Aunt Fanny remembered the names of the slave or little boy. It is just possible that someone may remember stories about a Black, circuit-riding preacher in Arkansas about 1890. I have put out a couple of feelers.

Chapter 6

The Earliest Colonizers
and the Last Awful Story

BY the time I had copied these stories, I was getting long in the tooth myself, so in my turn, I started sending archival material to my younger daughter (Aylwyn), who had surprised me by showing a strong interest in the family history, especially (as an ardent feminist) in the Scotts, my mother's family. I have not pursued the Scotts as deeply as I have the Vinsons.

Suffice it to say here that one of my great-grandfathers, Thomas Jefferson Scott, came from a slave-owning family and joined a Confederate Missouri regiment during the Civil War ("doin' the Wah," in local dialect), where he was mentioned in dispatches for signaling under fire at the Battle of Helena but remained a private throughout.

After the war, he settled in Coldwater, Mississippi, about thirty-five miles south of Memphis. Aylwyn and I went there. The old part of town is quite pretty, with towering old trees casting welcome, deep shade in summer and houses going back at least to the late nineteenth century, some possibly earlier, and a little creek running through town. We puttered around in the records a little, but the real gem was the old cemetery where many of the Scotts are buried. Some of the trees there produced a strange round, yellowish, hairy fruit about the size of a softball. My daughter picked one up, and when we went to the café for lunch, we asked what the tree was called. The waitress didn't know, but one of the customers said the fruit was from a bow dock tree and that the wood made excellent bows, better even than yew.[1]

The Scotts owned a few slaves back in Tennessee, so they were prosperous, like the Williamses, but there are no surviving stories about them. I thought that this was odd, but Grandaddy Scott was deaf and not much of a talker. He died when I was about nine, and it was not until I was middle-aged that I asked my mother about Scott family stories. She said that she had once asked Grandaddy about his father and that he had started to tell her but burst into tears, and Grandmother Scott had told her not to ask any more questions.

Many years later, Aylwyn found out why. The story has nothing to do with race, but I tell it because of the light it throws on combat veterans and on what war does to them and their children.

Aylwyn went back to Little Rock by herself one winter and started going through the morgue (as the archive is called) of *The Arkansas Gazette*. The whole story, including the cock-and-bull story that Grandaddy told my mother, is too long to go into here, involving, as it does, the generation of the Mexican War (1846–48) and a trigger-happy Texas ancestor named Snell on Grandmother Scott's (née Hirshfield) side of the family.

The upshot of it is that Great-Grandfather Thomas Jefferson Scott (who conducted himself gallantly during the Battle of Helena), when he was about fifty, ambushed and murdered his boss in 1893 in a dispute over wages. His son, my grandfather, hired a lawyer who had him plead insanity because of the trauma he had suffered during the Civil War (in effect, PTSD, or soldier's heart, as it was then called). The jury found him guilty anyway, probably reasoning that T. J. (as we have come to call him) was nothing special. Everyone had had a tough war but didn't go around murdering people afterward—not White people, anyway. T. J. did twenty-one years in the Arkansas State Penitentiary. When he got

---

1. A friend tells me that he grew up near the town of Bois d'Arc (Bow Wood) in southwest Missouri.

out, Grandaddy helped him to get a small veteran's pension, but otherwise he became an unperson, and perhaps that explains why there aren't any Scott stories.

I was in for another surprise when I started researching the Vinsons again. I have already mentioned that my father had believed that the Vinsons had been too poor to own slaves. When I checked the census record for 1860, it seemed to bear this out: both my first and second great-grandfathers Vinson were illiterate. But Great-Grandfather Exum (1838–1905) had been a lieutenant; he learned to read and write in the army, according to a letter from one of his comrades. His father, Jesse (my second great-grandfather, 1806–70), remained illiterate, a smallholder on Bear Swamp, a few miles southeast of Jackson.

Jackson is on the south edge of the Great Dismal Swamp, which in early colonial times covered more than one million acres. Today, it stretches about nineteen miles east to west and about twenty-two or twenty-three miles north to south (from Sudbury, North Carolina, almost to Portsmouth, Virginia). The land is dotted with what appear to be mostly small cotton farms. Bits of cotton still stuck to the plants in December when my older daughter and I visited. The farms were cut up into smallish plots by bayous and creeks. While bayous have no current, the creeks once powered the many mills that dotted the area. We found Barlow's Mill Pond (once Wheeler's Mill), where Exum enlisted for the Civil War,[2] but looking for Jesse's land was too much of a challenge: it was on Potecasi Creek, but the boundaries are marked in the old documents by gum and pine trees and "a gum in a branch"—i.e., a gum tree in a creek. We might have been able to translate this into modern terms, but we did not have time. The ever-helpful Mrs. Roye sent me a copy of a map, which I kept, but not until this year (2020) did I realize how important it would prove.

Neither Jesse nor Exum had owned slaves, but my problem was to go beyond Jesse. Finally, I joined Ancestry.com, and the

2. When I stopped to ask directions, an African American man answered the door. For once, I was tactful enough not to explain why I was looking for the pond.

floodgates opened. Jesse's father may have been a man named David (1767–1831) who had a dozen children but not much money. In my cynical moments, I imagine that if he had farmed more and romanced his wife less, he could have left his children in better financial shape. On the other hand, I tend to be romantic myself, so I'm glad that David (if that's who it was) had so much success with his wife. So far, I haven't found any slaves in his record.

I still do not know for sure who Jesse's father was. Mrs. Roye was stymied, too, when we wrote during the early 1990s. I have been in correspondence with a genealogist in North Carolina (our families seem to have been neighbors on Bear Swamp in the nineteenth century), Mr. Kenneth Odom, but he hasn't found Jesse's father either.

At the earlier end of the family, one of the Vinson descendants in the Ancestry network put me on to a Thomas Vinson Jr. Following up hints about him led me to John Brayton's books on the first families of North Carolina.[3] I shall take the entries in chronological order.

Brayton believes that the earliest known member of the family ("the progenitor") was John, a tailor, "the father of Thomas Vinson, Sr. and grandfather of Thomas Vinson, Jr. of Chowan and Northampton Counties, NC." John had an unclear but close relationship with a Captain William Corker (who left him fifty pounds in his will) which seems to have involved land dealings and possibly slaves. Most entries simply record him as a "tithable"—i.e., someone who could be taxed.[4]

We know almost nothing about Thomas Sr. (whose will has been lost). We may guess that he was born about 1650. He is listed in the quitrents of Prince George County, Virginia, in 1704.[5] We have a few records of land dealings by his son and widow, Sarah, which indicate that he grew tobacco and was well-to-do, but dead

3. See Brayton, *Registry of Ancestors* and *Ancestor Biographies*.

4. Brayton, *Registry of Ancestors*, 509.

5. "Quitrent" (as I discovered in a massive old dictionary) is an old feudal term for money paid to a lord in lieu of physical labor—e.g., road mending or the like (*Webster Third International Dictionary* [1967], s.v. "Quitrent").

by 1716. No slaves of his are mentioned. Thomas Sr. and Sarah lived in Surry County or perhaps Charles City County, Virginia, probably east of Richmond and south and north of the James River, respectively.[6] Two centuries later, this area would be bitterly fought over in the Peninsular Campaign during the Civil War.

Thomas and Sarah's son, Thomas Jr., was born around 1690 and died between January 15, 1762, when he dictated his will, and February 1764, when it was finally probated. Thomas Jr. mentions one slave in his will, but as he left a total of 710 acres plus money and livestock to his wife, Isobel, and children, I have to assume that he owned enough slaves to farm all of that, which would have been a lot of people, though I cannot guess how many.[7]

Or perhaps not so many. He might have used English indentured servants, or both them and slaves. Daniel Defoe has Moll Flanders speak of the equivalence of slaves and indentured servants in so many words: they are bought and sold (as Moll is), their quality is "despised," and those transported for life were branded with the initial letter of their crime before they left England.[8] Both Zinn and Isenberg make clear that there was no significant distinction between Black slaves and White indentured servants.[9] It was a shock to learn that the Vinsons had been so wealthy and owned slaves at such an early date, with, presumably, all the cruelty and neglect that slavery implies.

These few facts about the Thomas Vinsons raise all sorts of questions about why the Vinsons moved to the colonies in the first place. What did they hope to gain? And, of course, this raises questions in turn about where they came from—England, clearly, but where? If Thomas Sr. was born about 1650, that was just a few years after the chaos of the English Civil War, the execution of Charles I in 1649, and the Protectorate under the rule of the Cromwells.

6. Brayton, *Registry of Ancestors*, 509.

7. Brayton, *Ancestor Biographies*, 225.

8. Defoe, *Moll Flanders*, 274: "We were both on board, actually bound to Virginia, in the despicable quality of transported convicts destined to be sold for slaves."

9. Zinn, *People's History*, 44; Isenberg, *White Trash*, chaps. 1–3.

Thomas would have been nearly forty by the time of the Glorious Revolution in 1688, when England became a Commonwealth and established its Bill of Rights. Wealthy men might have sided with the king, but not necessarily. Which side were the Vinsons on, and how did English politics at home influence their decision to move to the New World? What did they do during Bacon's Rebellion (1676), that brief solidarity of Whites, slaves, women, and White indentured servants put down by armed might not of the colony's militia but of regulars sent from England?

What did English politics really mean to the colonists, anyway, who had to deal with swamps, poisonous snakes five feet long,[10] cougars, and bears, and who had to negotiate with or fight Native Americans?[11] Given their wealth, the Vinsons' ownership of slaves—probably a lot of slaves—and/or indentured servants was hardly a surprise. What, then, happened to their wealth between Thomas Jr. and illiterate smallholder Jesse, my second great-grandfather?

Thomas Jr. and Isobel had seven sons and four daughters. At some point, they moved to Northampton County, now in North Carolina, and bought land around Bear Swamp on Potecasi Creek, southeast of Jackson.[12] One son, James (1735–90), did very well for himself, becoming a wealthy planter and slave owner and sheriff of Northampton County. James had a son named David (1767–1831), and if this was Jesse's father, then I am descended from him.

At all events, Jesse owned about 144 acres of land around Bear Swamp near Potecasi Creek. Mrs. Roye has sent me the names of other Vinsons, also landowners in the area, and they all seem to be children or brothers of Thomas Jr. and James, so I cannot but feel that I must be related to them. But for the moment, that's as

10. Personal observation.

11. For a hilarious send-up of the adjoining colony of Maryland and its politics, see Barth, *Sot-Weed Factor*, chap. 10.

12. Isenberg, *White Trash*, chap. 2, has a lengthy and bleak account of life in early North Carolina, which split from Virginia, with its own charter, in 1663.

far back as I can go, so it is now time to return to Exum and move forward from him.

I have already discussed the career of Jesse's son, Exum, my first great-grandfather. My great-aunts and Cousin Katherine told me several stories about him. From these stories and the written record, he seems to have been an ambitious man with an explosive temper. Once, the circus came to his adopted town, Augusta, Arkansas, on the White River, about forty miles north of Little Rock. Naturally, there was a parade, so Exum left his store to watch it and sat down on a keg that someone had left in front of his store. Some of his acquaintances, watching him, knew that he had a morbid fear of snakes (not surprising for a barefoot country boy who had grown up wary of rattlers and cottonmouths), so they told him that the circus's snake charmer was keeping his snakes in that keg. Exum jumped up in terror, ran into his store to get his pistol, and had to be restrained from shooting the snake charmer for leaving his snakes where he (Exum) could sit on them.

Exum's wife, Molly, also had a temper. Although Exum had been ambitious as a young man, his energy apparently declined a good deal as he aged (war takes a lot out of you). He seems to have spent a lot of time at his store playing checkers. This annoyed Molly, who wanted him to pay more attention to business. "I have to do everything, from feeding the stock to winding the clock," she complained. She used to roar into the store like Jesus among the money changers, tear the checkerboards in half, throw the pieces into the street, and scold her husband publicly.

Their oldest son, Baldy Sr., my grandfather (1867–1917), inherited his parents' temper. One newspaper obituary says that "reflection upon him or his, in matters of honor or honesty, meant insult; and insult meant fight, regardless of time, place or consequences."[13] Like his father and sister, Great-Aunt Blanche,[14]

13. My daughter sent me a copy of Grandpa Baldy's obituary. Someone got carried away with the scissors—there are no bylines, mastheads, or dates. Someone long ago cut a copy of this obituary out of a newspaper in Augusta, Arkansas, *The Free* . . . but the rest of the name has not survived.

14. Baldy Sr. and Aunt Blanche inherited their father's marksmanship. She owned a .44 Smith and Wesson with which, in her youth, she could pop the

Baldy Sr. was a crack shot, once hitting over 140 skeet in a row (his friends presented him with a Remington five-round twelve-gauge, full choke). He was a brilliant lawyer, too, once earning the highest fee that any lawyer in Arkansas had earned up to that time, and was active in all manner of business enterprises. He was more open-minded than a lot of White men at the time, being one of the few lawyers in the state who took Black clients.

My grandparents Baldy Vinson Sr. and Mary Lynn Vinson

But alcoholism cut him down. In 1903, a year after his oldest son was born and a little over a year before my father and aunt were born, Baldy Sr. was involved in a shooting affray with two Black men, Henry Johnson and Ed Coleman, possibly over a Black woman, Ella McDowell, who was wounded in the back (jealousy? a stray bullet?). Johnson and Coleman also allegedly killed one White man and wounded another. The shootings took place in a saloon in Lake Village, Arkansas (where Baldy Sr. had an office, and where he and Grandmother lived for a time), around two on a November morning (contemporary newspapers muddle the date). Baldy Sr. was shot twice and was not expected to live, though he did. Ed Coleman got away, but Henry Johnson was arrested. But by noon, a mob broke into the jail, took Johnson to the center of town, and lynched him, leaving his body hanging in the middle of town until about five in the afternoon.

---

head off a running chicken at fifty feet.

Grandpa's story has all the earmarks of a whorehouse brawl. While I do not know the exact circumstances, of course, the mingling of races and sexes in a bar at two in the morning in Arkansas in 1903 suggests that the White men were there for no good purpose. It could have been worse. In one Arkansas town (I have lost the reference), the sheriff tried to protect his prisoner. The mob tied them face to face, lynched them, set them on fire, and left the bodies to rot in the middle of the street.

There is often a strong sexual element to racial violence. In the South, the emotions aroused by the thought of sex between Black and White are powerful, irrational, and complex, as Dr. Jacoway notes.[15] At bottom (and behind a lot of lynchings) is the fear that Black men want sex with normally unattainable White women and, worse, that White women might enjoy it, a fear that Robert Mapplethorpe's photographs of interracial couples and homoeroticism have done nothing to allay. On the other hand, the illicit is always especially attractive, so the White man, especially a married White man, who seeks out Black women is wracked by both pleasure and guilt. If a Black man breaks the color bar, that is miscegenation, what Senator Eastland of Mississippi called the "mongreliz[ation] of the Anglo-Saxon race."[16] But because the White man is superior (in his own eyes), *his* breaking of the color bar is never miscegenation but a privilege that he is entitled to. Therefore, "social equality," women's rights, integration—all threaten the White man's sexual freedom and limit the scope of his conquests.

My father never talked about his father or saved any correspondence or newspapers, because it was all too painful for him (Baldy Sr.'s shameful behavior continued until his death). But Jimmy told my mother (who told me) that his father commonly frequented Black bars and that when he and my grandmother first married, he often tried to persuade her to go partying with him, but she refused. It is common for alcoholics to seek out cheap bars (and the women they find there), but most give it up after a brush

15. See Jacoway, *Turn Away Thy Son*, 359–62.
16. Jacoway, *Turn Away Thy Son*, 359.

with death, especially after causing someone else's death. Baldy Sr., however, kept up his drinking and womanizing for another fourteen years, until he died of pneumonia during a drunk. Grandmother Vinson locked him out of the house but loved him to the end. "I think Baldy's a lovely name," she told my mother.

So, there you have it. My children and I are descended from traffickers in probably White and certainly Black human beings from as long as 370 years ago—from Confederate soldiers, at least one Klansman, and a rounder who caused the lynching of a Black man. As a group, the Vinson men are violent, with a tendency toward alcoholism.

Cousin Katherine put it best: "The Vinson men are all looking for something. They don't know what it is, but they're looking for it anyway."

What we were looking for, of course, was God. Exum and Molly had been Methodists but quarreled with the minister over dancing and joined the Baptists instead. Exum's tombstone attests to his love of God. Grandmother Vinson sent her children to the Presbyterian church "as a matter of convenience," she said. My father interpreted that to mean getting them out of the house on Sunday morning so she and Baldy Sr. could have a little peace and quiet.

Immigrants to the early colonies had to swear allegiance to the Church of England, so John must have done so in the 1640s or '50s, but otherwise, there is little record of attendance or belief until I came along.[17]

As a little boy, I sometimes attended the Methodist Sunday school or church, because my friend Bronson Jacoway did and because Mrs. Benson, our fifth-grade teacher in public school, kept an attendance record on our classroom blackboard (long before the Supreme Court ruled in Murray v. Curlett). I went often enough to earn a Bible (in Tom Sawyer fashion) signed by the minister, Dr.

---

17. I found a passenger list dated 1635 for the Primrose, bound for "Virginea," on Ancestry.com. The passengers (all men) were examined and sworn by the minister at Gravesend. There is a Thomas Vinson among them, but I have nothing to connect him with Brayton's John Vinson or his descendants.

Walton. I took it home and sat down to read it, but the naughty bits were over my head (Well, of course Adam knew his wife! They were married, weren't they?). I bogged down in the "begats" and then put it aside and forgot about it.

When I sobered up in 1979, I did some serious reflection on just what I believed and why as a means to staying sober. It was clear that something about which I knew nothing was keeping me and the many others in my support group sober and, ever so slowly, improving my relationships with other people. I supposed I could call that God.

It never occurred to me to go to church or talk to a minister, though I encountered several at meetings of my support group. Then, in 1986, I joined Southside Presbyterian Church, under the pastorate of Rev. John Fife, in good trouble because of the Sanctuary Movement, as I have explained above. I went to Southside, and, as I got to know Jim and Pat Corbett, I went to the Quaker meeting. At both, I learned about liberation theology and the Gospels, about the Constantinian captivity, and about the kinship of imperial Rome and imperial America.

My theology still needs the simplicity of the child or sharecropper. I cling to the Gospels, though Saint John seems a bit of a mystic; Saint Paul is a Johnny-come-lately. But I can handle Amos and the Synoptic Gospels. God and Jesus call us to love everyone, difficult as that may be. Amos tells us to do justice, love mercy, and to be humble (mindful, I suppose, that we are not always loveable ourselves). That's as much as I can handle.

To return to the family, I learned about the lynching in the '90s, when a cousin by marriage (a former Navy computer expert in anti-submarine warfare) tracked me down and sent me copies of newspaper articles from Pine Bluff (between Lake Village and Little Rock) and from Arlington, Texas, where he lives. No member of my family in Arkansas, not even Cousin Katherine, ever breathed a word of it. Probably, they just didn't know—the computer expert is quite capable of digging up old newspaper accounts on his own. The time of his discovery was long before talk (among Whites, at least) of accounting or reparations. But now, even if I could find the families of Henry Johnson and Ella McDowell 120 years later, what reparations could I make? All I can see to do is to acknowledge and take up my burden of guilt. In the end, I have decided to contribute to historically Black Philander Smith College, as my parents did.

We not only owe reparations to our African American slaves and their descendants but to the White indentured servants whom Thomas Sr., Thomas Jr., and James essentially enslaved during the seventeenth and eighteenth centuries. Remember that convicted White indentured servants were branded in England, and their contracts in the colonies could be sold, which, effectively, was selling and buying the person. For this and other reasons, I contribute to the American Civil Liberties Union.

Chapter 7

No Trumpets Blew

I N telling this story, I fear that I have not given my parents enough credit. They broke the cycle of racism intertwined with violence (the only thing that supports racism). They chose to be educated in the North (my father worked his way through Wharton, with some help from his uncle), then they took that education back home to Little Rock and made it mean something. They sent their children to be educated in the North, and we, in turn, have sought to teach our children and others. They did not talk about kindness and decency; they lived those qualities, and I hope that sometimes, I have lived up to their example.

My father, James Russell Vinson

My mother, Louise Scott Vinson

I want to go back to election night of 1992. On that night, Bill Clinton from Hope, Arkansas, was elected president of the United States. He wasn't our greatest president, but he was pretty good, and although he had extramarital affairs, that's no more than Wilson, Franklin Roosevelt, and Kennedy did before him.[1] He brought in a large budget surplus, and he didn't let the economy crash. Though he shot off a couple of whizbangs at the Middle East, he didn't start a war there, and generally, we felt pretty safe and prosperous in his hands. Besides, we got Hilary as well as Bill, and Bill might agree that she's the better man of the two. I've always trusted her, because she worked at the Rose Law Firm. The original firm was Rose, Meek, House, Baron, and Nash, and Archie House (one of the founding partners) was my parents' attorney and the attorney for the Little Rock school board, which stood up to Faubus during the integration crisis.

So, Arkansas's first president canceled the hillbilly, rebel-yelling stereotype that Arkansans were saddled with for so long. I watched the results on television that night. A quiet, respectful crowd gathered in front of the handsome Old State House on East Markham Street.[2]

---

1. Republicans, except possibly for Harding, are much less interesting in this respect. I disregard the twice-impeached occupant.

2. The Old State House exemplifies Palladian restraint, whereas the present

The Old State House, Little Rock

There were no Confederate battle flags or rebel yells, and no one sang "Dixie." Lady Baxter, a siege cannon from Reconstruction, rested quietly on her trunnions and listened to the crowd sing "America the Beautiful." I felt an enormous sense of rest and relief. I felt that we, both Arkansas and America, had made a lot of progress.

Well, then we embarked on alternating decency and disasters. We had eight years of "Shrub" Bush, who did let the economy crash and started the pointless invasion of Iraq, the widespread and disastrous consequences of which the world is still dealing with. As if to atone for that, we elected Barack Obama, and for his first two years, it really seemed as if the United States was honestly struggling to make amends for its racist past. But then, in a shocking midterm reversal, we gave Obama a reactionary Republican congress.

Worse, in 2016, we elected Trump, who won the Electoral College (like "Shrub" Bush) but lost the popular vote twice, was impeached twice, and still encourages racism and violence as if he were a reincarnation of Jefferson Davis himself. In *The Guardian* of May 12, 2021, David Smith remarks the following of the current

---

capitol, closely modeled on the national capitol, exemplifies Michelangelesque grandeur.

impasse: "So Republican states legislatures will continue to use the false claims of fraud to justify new voting restrictions that disproportionately affect people of color."[3] It is all depressingly evocative of the post-Reconstruction, Jim Crow period.

Now, we have Biden, who is a fundamentally decent man but who, like Obama, is saddled with a divided Congress. The last twenty years have taught us only that we cannot take progress for granted—that it is as fragile as a butterfly wing and must be sheltered and protected for many decades. The history of voting rights alone shows that Americans may not be capable of such lengthy, sustained effort.

I have told my ancestors' stories not in chronological order but in the order in which I discovered them. It is incomplete, because I have not been able to chase down some important facts, like John Vinson's dealings in seventeenth-century Virginia or Jesse Vinson's parentage and Thomas Vinson Jr.'s relation to him, if any. But the broad outlines are clear: we are upper-class (well, upper middle-class), descended from wealthy traffickers in human beings, Black and White, exploiters of human labor. We must acknowledge and talk honestly about who we are and what we did, both as individuals and as a nation, or we are doomed to repeat our ancestors' cruel oppression.

As I prepare this manuscript for the editor, I have just learned of the juries' findings in the "Unite the Right" case in Charlottesville, Virginia, and in the Ahmaud Arbery case in Georgia. White supremacists and racist White men found guilty twice in the old Confederacy within a few days of each other! So, maybe there's hope.

---

3. Smith, "Liz Cheney's Ousting," para. 13.

Bibliography

Agee, James, and Walker Evans. *Let Us Now Praise Famous Men*. Boston: Houghton Mifflin, 1988.

"All Is Quiet at Lake Village—Sherrif Preston and Posse Cause the Leader to Leave." *Pine Bluff Daily Graphic*, July 23, 1899. https://chroniclingamerica. loc.gov/lccn/sn89051168/1899-07-23/ed-1/.

Ashmore, Harry S. *Arkansas: A Bicentennial History*. New York: Norton, 1978.

———. *An Epitaph for Dixie*. New York: Norton, 1958.

Barth, John. *The Sot-Weed Factor*. Toronto: Bantam, 1969.

Bosman, Julie, and Lauren Leatherby. "U.S. Coronavirus Death Toll Surpasses 700,000 Despite Wide Availability of Vaccines." *New York Times*, November 1, 2021. https://www.nytimes.com/2021/10/01/us/us-covid-deaths-700k.html.

Brayton, John A. *Order of First Families of North Carolina Ancestor Biographies*. Vol. 1, *The First Two Hundred*. Rev. ed. Baltimore, MD: Otter Bay, 2011.

———. *Order of First Families of North Carolina Registry of Ancestors*. Memphis, TN: Brayton, 2005.

Brewer, Vivion Lenon. *The Embattled Ladies of Little Rock: 1958–1963: The Struggle to Save Public Education at Central High*. Fort Bragg, CA: Lost Coast, 1999.

Carroll, Rory. "'So Far from God, So Close to the Us': Mexico's Troubled Past with its Neighbour." *Guardian*, February 1, 2017. https://www.theguardian. com/us-news/2017/feb/01/donald-trump-us-mexico-relations-history.

"Casey Jones." Bluegrass Lyrics. https://www.bluegrasslyrics.com/song/casey-jones/.

Chappell, Bill. "U.S. Border Agents Chased Migrants on Horseback. A Photographer Explains What He Saw." NPR, September 21, 2021. https:// www.npr.org/2021/09/21/1039230310/u-s-border-agents-haiti-migrants-horses-photographer-del-rio.

Cobb, Jelani. "Donald Trump Is Serious When He 'Jokes' about Police Brutality." *New Yorker*, August 1, 2017. https://www.newyorker.com/news/news-desk/donald-trump-is-serious-when-he-jokes-about-police-brutality.

Cooke, Kristina, and Ted Hesson. "What Are 'Sanctuary' Cities and Why Is Trump Targeting Them?" Reuters, February 25, 2020. https://www.reuters.com/article/us-usa-immigration-crime/what-are-sanctuary-cities-and-why-is-trump-targeting-them-idUSKBN20J25R.

Defoe, Daniel. *Moll Flanders*. New York: New American Library, 1981.

Dinesen, Isak. *Out of Africa: And Shadows on the Grass*. New York: Random House, 1961. https://onlinereadfreenovel.com/isak-dinesen/41843-out_of_africa_and_shadows_on_the_grass.html.

Dinnerstein, Leonard, et al. *Natives and Strangers: Blacks, Indians, and Immigrants in America*. 2nd ed. Oxford: Oxford University Press, 1990.

Doggett, Lloyd. "Timeline of Trump's Coronavirus Responses." March 2, 2022. https://doggett.house.gov/media/blog-post/timeline-trumps-coronavirus-responses.

"Dom Helder Camara Quotes." Goodreads. https://www.goodreads.com/work/quotes/6303490-dom-helder-camara-essential-writings.

Dyer, John P. *The Gallant Hood*. New York: Konecky & Konecky, 1950.

Federal Writers' Project. *Arkansas, A Guide to the State*. American Guide Series. New York: Hastings, 1941.

Foner, Eric. *Reconstruction: America's Unfinished Revolution, 1863–1877*. New York: History Book Club, 2005.

Fox, Brian. "U.S. Agents on City Streets. Can Trump Do That?" *Arizona Daily Star*, July 22, 2020.

Freedman, David H. "Millions of Angry, Armed Americans Stand Ready to Seize Power If Trump Loses in 2024." *Newsweek*, December 20, 2021. https://www.newsweek.com/2021/12/31/millions-angry-armed-americans-stand-ready-seize-power-if-trump-loses-2024-1660953.html.

Gelles, Karl, et al. "How Police Pushed Aside Protesters Ahead of Trump's Controversial Church Photo." *USA Today*, June 11, 2020. https://www.usatoday.com/in-depth/graphics/2020/06/05/george-floyd-protests-trump-church-photo-curfew-park/3127684001/.

Grandin, Greg, *The End of the Myth: From the Frontier to the Border Wall in the Mind of America*. New York: Metropolitan, 2019.

Griffith, D. W. *Birth of a Nation*. 2 hr., 13 min to 3 hr., 13 min. Epoch Producing Co., 1915.

Harris, Joel Chandler. *Uncle Remus*. Savannah, GA: Beehive, 1974.

Healy, Melissa. "Suicides and Overdoses among Factors Fueling Drop in U.S. Life Expectancy." *Los Angeles Times*, November 26, 2019. https://www.latimes.com/science/story/2019-11-26/life-expectancy-decline-deaths-of-despair.

Hoffman, Kathy. "AZ Schools Supt. Kathy Hoffman: Why Biden's Universal Pre-K Plan Is a Huge Deal." *Arizona Daily Star*, May 16, 2021. https://tucson.com/opinion/local/az-schools-supt-kathy-hoffman-why-bidens-universal-pre-k-plan-is-a-huge-deal/article_48d146a6-ba65-11eb-816d-a7a9b668c679.html.

Isenberg, Nancy. *White Trash: The 400-Year Untold History of Class in America*. London: Atlantic, 2017.

Jackson, Wilfred, dir. *Song of the South*. 1 hr., 34 min. RKO Radio Pictures, 1946.

Jacoway, Elizabeth. *Turn Away Thy Son: Little Rock, the Crisis that Shocked the Nation*. New York: Free Press, 2007.

Jakes, Lara, and Eileen Sullivan. "A Senior U.S. Diplomat to Haiti Resigns, Citing the Biden Administration's 'Inhumane' Deportation Policy." *New York Times*, October 19, 2021. https://www.nytimes.com/2021/09/23/us/politics/haiti-diplomat-resign-biden.html.

Klein, Naomi. "Naomi Klein: How Power Profits from Disaster." *Guardian*, July 6, 2017. https://www.theguardian.com/us-news/2017/jul/06/naomi-klein-how-power-profits-from-disaster.

Knappenberger, Ryan. "Arizona Near Top of States for Bills Aimed at Voting Rights, Limits." *Cronkite News*, April 26, 2021. https://cronkitenews.azpbs.org/2021/04/26/arizona-near-top-of-states-for-bills-aimed-at-voting-rights-limits/.

Levinson, Jonathan, et al. "Federal Officers Use Unmarked Vehicles to Grab People in Portland, DHS Confirms." NPR, July 17, 2020. https://www.npr.org/2020/07/17/892277592/federal-officers-use-unmarked-vehicles-to-grab-protesters-in-portland.

Maharidge, Dale, and Michael Williamson. *And Their Children after Them: The Legacy of "Let Us Now Praise Famous Men," James Agee, Walker Evans, and the Rise and Fall of Cotton in the South*. New York: Pantheon, 1989.

McCausland, Phil. "DeJoy Testifies before Congress, Commits to Delivering Election Ballots on Time." NBC News, August 21, 2020. https://www.nbcnews.com/politics/2020-election/dejoy-testifies-congress-commits-delivering-election-ballots-time-n1237674.

McGraw, Daniel. "How to Put 170,000 COVID Deaths in Perspective." *Bulwark*, August 20, 2020. https://www.thebulwark.com/how-to-put-170000-covid-deaths-in-perspective/.

Nevett, Joshua. "George Floyd: The Personal Cost of Filming Police Brutality." BBC News, June 11, 2020. https://www.bbc.com/news/world-us-canada-52942519.

Nolan, Rachel. "I've Lost Everything to the Beast." *New York Review*, May 13, 2021. https://www.nybooks.com/articles/2021/05/13/ms-13-el-salvador-lost-everything-beast/.

"One Negro Lynched." *Pine Bluff Daily Graphic*, November 4, 1903. https://chroniclingamerica.loc.gov/lccn/sn89051168/1903-11-04/ed-1/seq-1/.

Pilkington, Ed. "'These Are His People': Inside the Elite Border Patrol Unit Trump Sent to Portland." *Guardian*, July 27, 2020. https://www.theguardian.com/us-news/2020/jul/27/trump-border-patrol-troops-portland-bortac.

Rael, Patrick. "Died of a Theory." *Black Perspectives*, January 29, 2015. https://www.aaihs.org/died-of-a-theory/.

Randoph, Vance. *Pissing in the Snow and Other Ozark Folk Tales*. Urbana: University of Illinois Press, 1976.

"Rebalancing the 'COVID-19 Effect' on Alcohol Sales." May 7, 2020. NielsenIQ. https://nielseniq.com/global/en/insights/analysis/2020/rebalancing-the-covid-19-effect-on-alcohol-sales/.

Rivera, Suelen. "Arizona Has Third-Worst School System in the United States, per WalletHub." *KTAR News*, July 27, 2021. https://ktar.com/story/4593129/arizona-has-3rd-worst-school-system-in-the-united-states-per-wallethub/#:~:text=Arizona%20came%20in%20at%20No,highest%20quality%20of%20public%20education.

Roberts, Bobby Leon, and Carl H. Moneyhon. *Portraits of Conflict: A Photographic History of Arkansas in the Civil War*. Fayetteville, AR: University of Arkansas Press, 1987.

Romm, Tony, and Erica Werner. "State, Local Governments Wrestle over Quickly Dwindling Coronavirus Aid, Complicating Talks on Next Federal Bill." *Washington Post*, July 13, 2020. https://www.washingtonpost.com/us-policy/2020/07/13/cities-states-cares-act/.

Ronstadt, Linda. "Corrido de Cananea." Letras. https://www.letras.com/linda-ronstadt/374042/.

Simon, Steven, and Jonathan Stevenson. "How Can We Neutralize the Militias?" *New York Review*, August 19, 2021. https://www.nybooks.com/articles/2021/08/19/how-can-we-neutralize-militias/.

Smith, David. "Donald Trump Hints at Assassination of Hillary Clinton by Gun Rights Supporters." *Guardian*, August 10, 2016. https://www.theguardian.com/us-news/2016/aug/09/trump-gun-owners-clinton-judges-second-amendment.

———. "Liz Cheney's Ousting Proves the 'Big Lie' Is the Republican Party's Religion." *Guardian*, May 12, 2021. https://www.theguardian.com/us-news/2021/may/12/liz-cheney-ousting-republican-party-trump-big-lie.

Taylor, Tate. *The Help*. 2 hr., 26 min. Walt Disney Studios Motion Pictures, 2011.

Vinson, Sterling. "Fascism Creeps Up on You." *Sterling Analysis* (blog), February 23, 2020. https://sterlinganalysis.blogspot.com/.

———. "Los Tapiros." *Journal of the Southwest* 33.1 (1993) 34–51.

Woodward, Alex. "DeJoy's Postal Service Cuts Will Disenfranchise Mail-In Voters, 21 State Attorney Generals Warn." *Independent*, June 22, 2021. https://www.independent.co.uk/news/world/americas/us-politics/louis-dejoy-mail-cuts-voting-b1870714.html.

Woodward, C. Vann. *Mary Chestnut's Civil War*. New Haven: Yale University Press, 1981.

———. *The Strange Career of Jim Crow*. New York: Oxford University Press, 1955.

Zinn, Howard. *A People's History of the United States*. New York: Perennial Classics, 2001.

Zucotti, Susan. *The Italians and the Holocaust*. New York: Basic, 1987.

www.ingramcontent.com/pod-product-compliance
Lightning Source LLC
LaVergne TN
LVHW021610080426
835510LV00019B/2508